W9-BPZ-533

Spokane, WA 99203-3346

Whimsies & Whynots

A Playful Approach to Quiltmaking

Mary Lou Weidman

To Maxine ☺
"My adopted aunt"
You and your wonderful
family have provided
many memories that I
treasure. I look more you
and Clarence. I
I enjoy sharing my
stories and hope you
enjoyed this book.
Love to you,
Mary Lou ☺

That Patchwork Place®

THANK-YOUS

First of all, I thank God for providing me with a treasured gift. Every quilt idea and creative aspect has come directly from Him.

I am deeply grateful to all those who have helped make this book a reality. Thanks to:

That Patchwork Place. Skills provided by Melissa Lowe and Kerry Hoffman were greatly appreciated. Their skills, advice, and knowledge all helped bring this book together.

Sharon Evans Yenter, from In The Beginning. Thank you for believing in me, for your kindness and wisdom, and for sharing your wonderful family.

Judy Goodrich, who typed the manuscript and proofread my original. A big job, done well and with a wonderful attitude.

Pam J. Clarke, for her creative and artistic machine quilting. It is the best I have ever seen.

Julie Gruber Lynch and Kathy Skomer, for their creative support, kind hearts, and humor over the years.

Manya Powell, for friendship, advice, pattern corrections, and help assembling the "Creative Friends" quilts.

Sister Paula Turnbow, an artist and gifted teacher who touched me with her interest and knowledge.

Kari Pearson and k.p. kids, for their fabric samples and advice.

Gayle Snitselaar and Benartex, for their fabric samples.

Kaufman Fabrics, for the fabric samples they provided.

The many individuals who accepted my creative challenge and made a Creative Friend block.

My "Magpie" and "WSQ" quilt friends. How wonderful to have supportive and creative friends such as these.

The many kind and supportive shop owners I know, especially Annette, Diana, Jackie, Joan, JoAnna, RaeLynn, Rosalie, Sandy, and Stephanie.

Students Helen Klapp, Melody Coffey-Love, Tracy McHugh, Kelly Radcliff, Mollie Ressa, RaeLynn Roadhouse, Judy Smith, Sandy Sylvester, Kay Zellmer, and Terry Waldron for being my friends, inspirations, and advocates, and for keeping my mailbox and heart full.

Finally, thanks to the many students who continue to inspire me with their wonderful creative spirits.

CREDITS

EDITOR-IN-CHIEF	Kerry I. Hoffman
TECHNICAL EDITOR	Melissa A. Lowe
MANAGING EDITOR	Judy Petry
DESIGN DIRECTOR	Cheryl Stevenson
COPY EDITOR	Liz McGehee
PROOFREADER	Melissa Riesland
LINE ART ILLUSTRATOR	Mary Lou Weidman
TECHNICAL ILLUSTRATOR	Brian Metz
PHOTOGRAPHER	Brent Kane
TEXT AND COVER DESIGNER	Barbara Schmitt
PRODUCTION ASSISTANT	Claudia L'Heureux

DEDICATION

This book is dedicated to:

My grandmothers, Augusta Louise Lovick Flesberg and Louise Amalia Fisher Donahue, whose kindness, wisdom, and love of family, friends, and home were a wonderful example of what quilters can do and be;

My husband, Mark, who set aside his needs and provided support in all ways for my creative journey;

My children, Shari, Jason, and Shelbi, who are my inspirations and joy;

My mother, Geneva Donahue, for love and hours of binding and labeling quilts;

My father, Ted Donahue, for love and an appreciation for art and design, and especially for the hours he's spent looking for buttons at garage sales!

MISSION STATEMENT

WE ARE DEDICATED TO PROVIDING QUALITY PRODUCTS AND SERVICE BY WORKING TOGETHER TO INSPIRE CREATIVITY AND TO ENRICH THE LIVES WE TOUCH.

Whimsies & Whynots: A Playful Approach to Quiltmaking
© 1997 by Mary Lou Weidman
That Patchwork Place, Inc., PO Box 118
Bothell, WA 98041-0118 USA

Printed in South Korea
02 01 00 99 98 97   6 5 4 3 2 1

No part of this product may be reproduced in any form, unless otherwise stated, in which case reproduction is limited to the use of the purchaser. The written instructions, photographs, designs, projects, and patterns are intended for the personal, noncommercial use of the retail purchaser and are under federal copyright laws; they are not to be reproduced by any electronic, mechanical, or other means, including informational storage or retrieval systems, for commercial use.

The information in this book is presented in good faith, but no warranty is given nor results guaranteed. Since That Patchwork Place, Inc., has no control over choice of materials or procedures, the company assumes no responsibility for the use of this information.

Library of Congress Cataloging-in-Publication Data
Weidman, Mary Lou,
    Whimsies & whynots : a playful approach to quiltmaking / by Mary Lou Weidman.
        p.   cm.
    Includes bibliographical references.
    ISBN 1-56477-180-6
    1. Quilting. 2. Patchwork. 3. Creative ability. I. Title.
TT835.W445   1997
746.46'041—dc21   96-37092
                                                                    CIP

CONTENTS

"We are shaped and fashioned by what we love."

VINCENT VAN GOGH

DEAR FRIENDS,

We hear the word "creativity" used a lot, but many of us don't know what makes us creative or feel that we are creative. When I began quilting in 1974, I never dreamed that the traditional quilts I made from patterns my grandmothers gave me would lead me to create story quilts and, eventually, this book.

My journey into storytelling and creativity began in 1987, when I tired of the traditional quilts covering my beds, walls, and furniture. I wanted to use quilts to tell the little stories that amused me and my friends and family. I took many classes in my search to become more creative and to turn my ideas into quilts. But I didn't find exactly what I was looking for: the quilts I longed to sew. So I started the slow process of finding my own way through trial and error. To help, I read everything I could find on the creative mind.

How do we learn, or really relearn, to be creative? I think I learned the basic lessons and techniques in this book from my father, an artist, when I was young. I also had teachers through the years who encouraged my creativity. But as an adult, I still needed help to begin my creative journey.

Early in my teaching career, I noticed that my students, no matter how different, had the same questions and problems. They were interested in ideas, idea development, and how to go about putting more creative energy into their quilts, as well as a way to portray simple ideas or stories about themselves and others. So that's what this book is about—learning to use your creativity to share your ideas or tell stories in your quilts.

How can you as a quiltmaker become more creative? In Part One, there are lessons and an exercise to help you understand what makes us creative, what stops us from being creative, and how to use simple ideas and techniques to create unique and imaginative quilts.

What inspires you? Are you feeling uninspired? Too often, we're so busy that we don't see what is right in front of us. We need to look at our lives from a different perspective. An exercise I've included in Part Two is really a collection of eye-opening games I've played by myself and with friends and students.

Because I base most of my work on personal observations or experiences, Part Three contains the anecdotes or stories behind many of my quilts. Faith, family, and friends are my favorite themes. I hope these stories kindle your imagination.

Part Four provides simple "recipes" you can use to make your quilts more appealing and unique.

Finally, Part Five is about creative friends, how they are inspired to work creatively. This section gives you a challenge to use as a jumping-off point for creating your own story quilts.

I am excited for you. I know what these ideas can produce and the personal satisfaction you can gain from putting a bit of yourself into your work. I hope I can inspire you to create a quilt that will tell something special about you and that will draw the eyes of all who are lucky enough to see it!

Mary Lou Weidman

> "Shoot for the moon. Even if you miss
> it, you will land among the stars."
>
> LES BROWN

HOW TO USE THIS BOOK

We all have books where you can skim the technique instructions, then make a quick project. *Warning:* this isn't that kind of book! It's a mind-expanding workbook, which means you may need to spend some time thinking about what you've read. This book gives you permission to try new things and guides you toward a new way of thinking. Because our lives and creativity change from day to day, the ideas and exercises in this book will affect you differently at different times. That is the fun of creativity: it's totally unpredictable!

I encourage you to read, absorb, and ponder this material. You may want to keep a notepad close by so you can jot down things that sound fun or challenging to try or that may be roadblocks to your creativity. This is a wonderful way to discover things about yourself and the way you think and work. You may even discover new ways to leap over past stumbling blocks.

Don't expect to try or master everything at once. Pick something and concentrate on it for awhile, then move on to something else. I often try something, put it away when I get creatively stuck, then come back after I have worked on something totally different. This approach keeps me fresh. I never know how the quilts will turn out or what I will learn as I go. But I'm happy working on the quilts, and I'm content because I'm learning and growing. By using the material in this book, you can learn and grow creatively in your work, no matter what your style.

Getting Started

How do you get started? Wondering where to begin is often a good starting point. I once had a frustrated quilter tell me, "Creativity? Who needs it." Clearly, as we search for new techniques and new ways to use patterns, color, value, shapes, fabrics, and embellishments in our quilts, we do. If you approach this book with a creative spirit, nothing is hard because you have nothing to lose and everything to gain. I've found that creative quilters seem to:

- Love to imagine
- Have courage
- Be self-motivated
- Keep working—even when frustrated
- Be adventurous
- Ask "I wonder …" questions
- Be willing to laugh and be laughed at
- Take color risks
- Learn from mistakes
- Be willing to say "I can do better"

Set some time aside to daydream every day. Daydreaming helps with creative flow and is a good practice for imagination growth.

5

Love to Imagine

The more you think about great designs and color palettes, the more original your quilts will be. Try to take at least ten to fifteen minutes out of your day to imagine. It will help your day and help you become more imaginative. Varying what we already know is not only important but fun.

Have Courage

I've met many quilters who are afraid to try anything unknown or new for fear of what friends would say. It is nice to have the approval of those around us, but often we

won't get it until we stand alone. This was certainly true in my case. I found that if someone didn't care for my folk-art style, I was encouraged. I knew I was doing something different! Now these someones are taking my classes to learn how to tell their stories and how their creativity works.

Be Self-Motivated

Don't compare yourself to others. Stick with what you are doing, and don't worry about so-and-so who is quilting twelve stitches per inch or another so-and-so who is turning out twenty-five quilts a year. Concentrate on how great *you* are!

We all need to nurture the artist in us. Give yourself pats on the back and compliments. Encouraging yourself is worth more than empty praise from well-meaning friends who don't really "get it."

Keep Working— Even When Frustrated

Often, we give up on projects because we're frustrated or fear that what we're doing isn't working. Rather than give up, I try several things to save a project. First, I take a break. Second, I get another opinion. I ask family members or friends what they think. I try to ask specific questions like "What about my color? Is there enough value here? Can you understand this? If not, what could I do to make this clearer?" Don't ask someone who won't support you. If you need to reach out to someone you do not know that well, do it. There are a lot of creative people who would be flattered you asked.

Finally, if you are totally overwhelmed and frustrated, put this project away for awhile. Get it out in a month or so. By then, you should have new ideas and fresh eyes. Stick with it; you may end up with something special.

Be Adventurous

If you dare to be adventurous, the possibilities are nearly endless. When we think of the story about the old woman who lived in a shoe, for example, we have a definite mental image. In the real world, this image makes no sense. A shoe for a home? But nearly everyone who sees an old woman standing in front of a shoe will understand what you mean.

I've been buying patterns, fabrics, and embellishments for years. And for years, I used these strictly according to directions. No more! Now I add to patterns or mix different patterns together to create something new and great. Try mixing fabric and using embellishments in brave new ways. You can drill a hole in almost anything and embellish your quilt. The point is to use these things with creativity and originality.

Think about ways you can take something and make something new out of it or give it a new twist. All it takes is imagination and a willingness to be creative.

Ask "I wonder ..." Questions

The most creative quilters are those who ask themselves "I wonder what would happen if ..." as they work. When you ask this sort of question, you are challenging the known. Try this at the beginning and in the middle of your projects; you'll be surprised at the unique way your mind works and the ideas you discover.

Be Willing to Laugh and Be Laughed At

This is difficult. But if you can laugh at the creative side of your work, you will enjoy what you are doing much more. Laughing at yourself and sharing laughter with others is key to feeling good and being creative.

A special note to perfectionists: Quilting is not about being somber and perfect. If you are a perfectionist, lighten up. I live with two of you, and I've learned that a perfectionist's biggest fear is that someone will learn he or she isn't perfect. No one is perfect. If you can laugh at things, you will be more relaxed and creative.

Take Color Risks

If all your quilts coordinate with the rooms in your home, you probably aren't taking color risks or stretching your creativity. Most of us were taught to use "decorator" colors for our treasured quilts. We've spent a great deal of time trying to match the colors in our furniture and walls, and matching the quilt design to the room theme. To solve this problem, I make some quilts for decorating and some where I play with color.

Are you are one of those quilters who like to proclaim "I never use yellow or orange"? Perhaps you should give them a try. It could do wonders for your creativity quotient. The more you experiment and stretch yourself, the more you will enjoy experimenting and stretching.

Learn from Mistakes

We all make mistakes. The more creative quilts I make, the more I realize that not every idea is a good one. Some things are better done other ways and some things are better not started in the first place. When you make a mistake, don't get discouraged! Simply make some mental notes and move on. Mistakes are valuable resources if you remember them. (If you aren't making any mistakes, you probably aren't learning anything new.)

Be Willing to Say "I can do better"

With every quilt you make, you learn something new. Gradually, everything you learn becomes part of your unique style. When I finish a quilt, I critique it myself. I ask myself what I could have done better and what I need to remember for the next quilt. This is an honest and useful exercise. I don't beat myself up. I just make mental notes so I can do better the next time.

If you think you can, you can.
If you think you can't, you can't.

Stopping Before You Get Started

Many quilters come into my classes with everything needed to make a wonderful quilt. But somehow, something happens. Mumbling in the background, some of these quilters talk their way out of taking action. Here are the excuses I hear most often:

- I don't have enough experience to try that.
- I haven't done it that way before.
- I never use those colors.
- It won't match my living room or bedroom or …
- My friend tried that and it didn't work.
- I tried that and it didn't work.
- I don't want to take responsibility for the results.
- That's not my style.
- I am not feeling well today but I will get back to this and try … Honest. No, really!
- It just won't work.

Sound familiar? I've used a few of these myself. Can you see the self-doubt and negative thoughts? When we use these excuses, we're afraid of facing up to our own or other's expectations.

Don't let yourself get away with this. Tell yourself, "I am not going to let myself do this again. I can do this project. If I take it step by step, I won't disappoint myself. I will be happy with what I learned and the results. I can't grow unless I try, and trying will make me more creative and more productive."

You are too special and have too many quilts inside you to stop before you start! Watch what not using these excuses can do for you.

The Collector

Before we talk about creativity, I want to take a moment to talk about someone I call "the collector."

The collector has the best sewing machine; the best assortment of rulers, rotary cutters, mats, and gadgets; and, of course, the most fabric. Tons and tons of fabric. And she loves shopping for more. A new gimmick? She must have one or two immediately. She hasn't ever finished a project, although she takes lots of classes as well as workshops with the shining stars of the quilt world. Her cupboards are stuffed full of blocks, strips, half-made dolls, pillows, and special holiday patterns.

The collector spends so much time shopping and planning because it's safer. When she buys those beautiful fabrics, the clerks "Ooh!" and "Ah!" over her wonderful choices. Compliments over might-have-been quilts—this is good enough for the collector. If she were to cut up those beautiful fabrics, people might not approve of what she did with them. Better and safer to collect!

The collector is a great person to have for a friend because she has a good heart, as well as every book, magazine, and class handout known to the quilt world. She loves quilts, quilters, and recipes too. She is a pleaser.

Our friend, the collector, suffers from fear and lack of self-confidence. Deep down, she longs for someone to say, "Hey, it's OK, I will love what you do because you did it and I love you! Finish some of those great things and see how good it makes you feel."

If this is you, I have something to say: Once people see your finished projects, they'll be supportive and excited for you. All it takes is a little commitment, working one project at a time. And it will make you feel good! Have courage. We all love fabrics, books, and patterns, but they don't do any good if they are not used. And, you know, using them gives you an excuse to buy more.

PART ONE

CREATIVITY

Creativity. What is it? How can you as a quiltmaker become more creative? Studies have shown that we are born creative—open to new ideas and things around us. This is how we manage to learn to walk, talk, and do all the things we do at a young age. Children have a wonderful sense of creativity; their artwork is spontaneous, free, and fun.

Sadly, around age nine, we begin to compare our artwork to our peers' and listen to our peers', parents', and teachers' opinions. Around adolescence, we begin to do realistic representations rather than abstract ones. We turn to adults like our parents and teachers to encourage our efforts. If we don't receive encouragement, we begin to lose our creative, inventive selves.

If we don't renew and use our creativity, we begin to lose the ability to come up with unique and imaginative ideas. But by knowing more about creativity, we can renew our creative spirit and start thinking and doing more creative work.

The Components of Creativity

Part of renewing your creativity is understanding the components of creativity and how they influence your designs and color, fabric, embellishment, and quilting choices. It's never too late to be creative; all you have to do is take the first step!

The five components of creativity are:

- Intuitive: going beyond words and thought
- Inventive: discovering uniqueness
- Imaginative: involving inspiration/visualization/transformation
- Conceptual: using words and language to trigger creative impulses
- Synectics: connecting unrelated things

Intuitive Creativity

CAKE WALK

Sometimes you can grab a batch of fabrics and just know it will make up into something exciting and fun. Have you ever dreamt up a creative and appealing pattern or combination of shapes, but been unable to explain how you came up with the design? This type of creativity is exciting because it surprises us. Sometimes, we just know something or feel something that we can't explain. This is intuitive creativity.

Inventive Creativity

Every year, we see more unique and interesting approaches to quiltmaking: new techniques, block and quilt designs, fabric designs, fabric dyes, threads, and embellishments. Inventive creativity is simply taking something and making something new and different out of it. Inventive creativity is what gives us better medicine, improved cars, more efficient kitchens, and weirder fashions year after year.

> "A wise man will make more opportunities than he finds."
> VINCENT VAN GOGH

Imaginative Creativity

Imaginative creativity really refers to using your imagination. When you daydream or picture something in your mind's eye, you are using imaginative creativity. What do you think of when you hear familiar expressions like cakewalk, dancing shoes, or hog heaven? Do you remember how to "play pretend"? Pretending that teddy bears and dollies are drinking tea in a magic garden is one example of imaginative creativity. We were all good at playing this game as children. Imaginative creativity is an invitation to regain this concept of pretending, to imagine and build on the dreams and pictures in your mind's eye.

Conceptual Creativity

Conceptual creativity is taking a concept, notion, or idea and presenting it in a new way. We envision and translate these concepts, notions, and ideas based on who we are. Don't worry that your quilt designs will be just like someone else's. No two people envision and translate ideas in the same way. If Edgar Allan Poe and Agatha Christie wrote about their experiences at the same party, I guarantee their stories would be completely different. Each of us has our own slant.

Conceptual creativity can be applied to any concept, from math and sciences to poetry, music, language, and dance. Transforming these ideas and images into quilt designs is another example of conceptual creativity. The fox-trot, minuet, and jitterbug dances are good examples of conceptual creativity.

Synectics as Creativity

Synectics means unifying or connecting unrelated things. If you pick a theme, grab different fabrics, add shape through appliqué or piecing, and quilt your work as a unit, you are using synectic creativity. A quilt challenge with a theme and a variety of fabrics is an exercise in synectic creativity.

"Don't be afraid to take a big step if one is indicated;

you can't cross a chasm in two small jumps."

DAVID LLOYD GEORGE

Creativity Stoppers

There are some things that actually hinder creativity; I call these "creativity stoppers." When it comes to our thinking process, old habits die hard. As you explore your creativity, look out for the following creativity stoppers and try to unlearn what you already know:

- There is only one right answer.
- Do it the right way.
- Don't ask questions.
- Don't make mistakes.
- Don't take risks.
- Stick with what you know.

VEILED THREAT

There Is Only One Right Answer

For years, we've been told there is only one right answer. The teacher asks a question with a specific answer in mind. If you provide that answer, you are rewarded. Because this starts at a young age, we are conditioned to mimic what the teacher says, portrays, and projects.

In quiltmaking, if your teacher says that no other quilter is as good as so-and-so, you nod and agree while taking her class. In other words, the right answer would be to imitate so-and-so's quilting style.

To be creative, we need more than one approach to each idea. You can't be very flexible if you have only one approach, and your quilts won't be as interesting as they could be.

Do It the Right Way

Another creativity stopper is doing things "the right way." We need to do many things the right way in life. As mature adults, we have many standards already set for us. If we do certain things right, we are rewarded with good lives and relationships. Additionally, we save a lot of time by doing things the right way.

Worrying about doing things the right way when trying to be creative makes taking risks impossible. Right-way thinking says that dogs aren't bigger than houses or that women aren't blue or that the sun doesn't have a big smile on its face. Creative thinking says "Why not?" You would be surprised how people respond to these creative approaches. Those who are more creative appreciate these touches. A smiling sun is much more interesting than a sun that just sits there. Breaking out of right-way thinking actually makes us more creative.

Don't Ask Questions

Some people pride themselves on being practical and realistic. While this is great for dealing with everyday challenges, there is no place for it in creativity. This is where "I wonder …" questions come into play. I have a friend who pointed out that I'm always asking "I wonder …" I guess I do say that a lot. I wonder … questions can lead to fun quilts and stories. Ask yourself questions like "I wonder what a garden that grew hats would look like? I wonder what pigs would look like if they flew? I wonder what a scarecrow made of vegetables would look like?" Asking questions leads to original ideas.

Don't Make Mistakes

Don't make mistakes. How often do we think this? To *do* something different is often construed as making a mistake. To *say* something different is often thought rude or irreverent. To offer a different answer is risky and something most of us are not brave enough to do. "If I say that," we think, "they'll think I'm wrong or strange or they won't understand." It seems better not to rock the boat.

Students say, "Would it be OK if I did such and such?" Of course it would be OK. It might be creative or a new avenue for you as a student. It doesn't matter whether you are in a class or a quilt guild. If you are trying to think creatively and your teacher or friends are saying "No, no, no," then you need to look elsewhere for encouragement. If you don't allow yourself to make mistakes, you cannot become more creative and innovative. It's safe, but dull. Failure gives you new ideas and viewpoints.

Don't Take Risks

Stretch your risk factor. Many people think play is immature and a waste of time. And play can be risky if you are worried about the opinions of others. When you play, your defenses are down. To get around this, stop worrying about being wrong or making a mistake. Remember: There is no wrong answer! Bringing out your playful side opens you up to innovative quilt ideas.

Stick with What You Know

Don't limit yourself. As quilters, we have strong opinions about what is good (i.e., acceptable) and what is not. Traditional quilters tend to argue that their style is the only style that counts; after all, it's based on our heritage. Contemporary quilters respond that their style is more art worthy. Other quilters argue over hand versus machine quilting. Everyone feels that the type of quilts they produce should be recognized as the best. Quilt judges and critics get caught up in this debate too.

It is easier to learn a style and stick with it than to experiment, so we're often uncomfortable trying new styles and methods. But breaking out of a style is a creativity-freeing effort. Take a new type of quilting class or buy a book that explains something totally new. Learn a new twist or add a twist on a traditional theme. You open yourself up to more creative ideas when you experiment.

Remember that the most prestigious quilt collectors and museum curators look for unique quilts—wonderful, one-of-a-kind quilts. Personal snippets and hidden messages give a quilt greater interest and value than workmanship alone. These quilts shout "Look at me!" You may make dozens of projects—all designed by someone else. Wouldn't it be fun to see one you designed and planned? Think of these quilts as stories waiting to be told. Share your story and the experiences that are yours alone.

Creativity Exercise

Many of us learned to sew with a pattern in front of us. We're fortunate to have so many patterns and books to choose from. Never in the history of quilting has there been such a variety of written materials, as many tools, or so much fabric. As the popularity of quilting demonstrates, we love to create those wonderful quilts to snuggle under, show off, admire, and hang.

But wait! There is so much more. If we dare to be creative, we can tell the special stories that are as individual as each person. Nearly everyone wants to share their thoughts and experiences and to have them count and be of value. Many of us would like to transfer these feelings to cloth, but are not sure where and how to start.

One of the best ways to start planning a quilt story is to use what I call verbal spark plugs—word clues to get your creative motor going. I've listed some of my favorite spark plugs below. Think about what you would do with each of these in a quilt.

We hear these sorts of word clues every day, but we usually don't think about what these could mean creatively. As you practice working with conceptual creativity, you will become more aware of creative themes and how to translate these themes into quilts your viewers will understand instantly. Once you've played with these, you should be warmed up and ready to talk about inspiration.

COAT OF ARMS

angleworm
bad apple
banana boat
barn owl

COFFEE BREAK

bat boy
bee's knees
Bible Belt
blue moon
bookworm
broken heart
busy bee
cakewalk
car coat
carrot top
cat's pajamas
catwalk
chain gang
chatterbox

checkered past
coat of arms
coffee break
coffee table
color guard
cookbook
crab apples
dancin' shoes
dinner bell
dog days
fairy tales
fat cat
flower child
fly fishing
fox trot
fruit fly

Horse Shoes

ghost writer
hairy ride
headband
hog heaven
horse shoes
hot dog
hot lips
jitterbug
lazy daisy
lucky duck
mental giant
mind games
paper boy
paper lion
patty-cake
pigheaded
pillow fight

pup tent
puppy love
queen bee
rat pack
road hog
shoe tree
shoo (shoe) fly
shoptalk
shutterbug
smart aleck
snapping turtle
straight arrow
sun belt
tea cozy
teatime
threadbare (bear)
tourist trap
tow (toe) truck
veiled threat
watchdog
watched pot

PART TWO

INSPIRATION

What inspires you? Are you feeling uninspired? The *New Webster's Dictionary* describes inspiration as "the creative impulse of an artist, inhaling." I like the idea of describing inspiration as inhaling. We're often so busy exhaling what we learned or thought that we forget to inhale what is right in front of us. Learning to inhale could make an enormous difference in your creative work!

I often hear students and friends say that they have trouble inspiring themselves. I'm convinced this is a learned response. If we look at the world around us with our day-to-day blinders on, we don't see it at all. We need to learn to see our world with open eyes, as children or tourists see it. Have you ever noticed how different things seem after you've been ill? Sometimes, after you've been sick, you view the world in a whole new way.

Really, there are many ways to be inspired. This is what makes creating so fun and inviting. Following is an exercise to help you learn how to "inhale" the world around you. This works well for me and has been helpful to both friends and students. I encourage you to do this as a game with friends or family members. If you challenge friends and other quilters around you, you often get a better variety of ideas and images.

If you are like most quilters, you have already studied the quilts. Most of us are visual; we are inspired by what we see. If you read the text before studying the quilts, you are verbal. Knowing this can give you new insights into the way you work.

Inspiration Exercise

Carry a piece of paper or notebook with you at all times and write down as many quilt themes as you can. (I keep a notebook in my purse, another in my travel bag, and yet another in my car.) Your creative flow will amaze you!

♥ Study the branches of trees. Did you notice that some branches go up and some go down? How could you use this in your quilting and patchwork designs? How does the foliage add to or take away from the stance of the tree? What kinds of things or people lean up against trees? What are stories that involve

"A person can be on the right track, but they'll get run over if they just stand there."
WILL ROGERS

trees? What grows on trees that could be the subject of a quilt?

♥ Find ten things shaped like a square. Architecture and buildings provide lots of ideas, of course, but did you consider taillights on cars? What other ideas can you see? How about lamps, furniture, perfume bottles, and other things indoors? How about sporting goods or hobbies that deal with squares? How could you work these square things into pieced quilt blocks?

♥ From a bowl of fruit, select a single piece and study it. Study the contours, shadows, curves, and colors. Return that piece to the bowl and study the contours, shadows, curves, and colors of all the fruit. How would the bowl of fruit look if it were made from squares or triangles? Smell the fruit and, while enjoying the taste, think of ways you could cut those shapes from fabric and use them in a quilt.

♥ Think of ten kinds of hats and the roles people wearing them play. How are these hats embellished? How could you tell a story using hats? I think hats are tremendously inspiring.

♥ Have you ever thought about all the things hands do? How many things can you think of that involve the use of hands? How could you tell a story using hands?

♥ Put on your favorite music and close your eyes. Let your mind wander to find ideas. *Hint:* The type of music you listen to may determine whether you are inspired to create a fabric masterpiece or a fun little quilt that makes you smile.

♥ Look for shapes of people and things in the clouds. This childlike task is a good way to get in a playful, creative mood. Try to think of themes based on what you see in the clouds. This is a great way to come up with fresh ideas.

♥ Challenge yourself to read about things you don't know a lot about. After we leave school, we tend to focus on our main interests only. When was the last time you went to the library and took out a book on poetry? Poetry touches our hearts and spirits. What better way to inspire a great quilt story?

♥ Watch children at a park or playing in their yards. See how they run and relate to other children and animals? Study their body movement and language—from jumping to bending down to pet the family dog. Aren't children's motions just full of stories?

❤ Think of a faraway place, one you haven't had the chance to visit. What do you think the people are like? What are the sights, smells, and sounds? Are animals and flowers part of this faraway place? Are there beautiful colors and interesting coins and tapestries? What stories would this land tell?

❤ Pick a person from history and pretend they came to visit for an evening or a day. What would you serve and who would you invite? What kind of activity could be involved? My husband has remarked he would play ball with Babe Ruth. What questions would you ask this person? What would you share? What items could be included in a quilt based on this idea?

❤ Think about the term "sweet dreams." What could this term mean in the best sense of the idea? What dreams would be sweet to you, to your dog, to a treasure hunter, or to a child the night before Christmas? What wonderful ideas can you come up with?

❤ Words can play an important role in inspiration. How many phrases with the word "love" can you come up with? How could this inspire you to create a quilt? Try other words and phrases. How about phrases with the word "apple"? Apple pie. Big apple. Apple dandy. Try words like sky, tree, laugh, or pear-pare-pair. You get the idea.

"Change starts when someone sees the next step."

WILLIAM DRAYTON

PART THREE

THE QUILTS & THEIR STORIES

Because I base most of my work on personal observations or experiences, I have included the anecdotes or stories behind many of my quilts. Each is a little piece of history. Interests change as do our lives and the people and places we are involved with. Faith, family, and friends are my favorite themes. Including things and people you love is what makes your quilts special.

"Laughter translates into any language."

GRANDMA DONAHUE

You Are the Sun, Moon, and Stars to Me
by Mary Lou Weidman, 1994,
Spokane, Washington, 70" x 89".
Machine quilted by Pam Clarke.

YOU ARE THE SUN, MOON, AND STARS TO ME

A few Christmases ago, I opened a little box containing a pretty pair of gold earrings with dangling stars, moon, and sun. On the attached card, my husband had written, "To Mary. You are the sun, the moon and the stars to me." I saved the card and enjoyed wearing the earrings. When we celebrated our twenty-fifth wedding anniversary, I took the theme and made this quilt, which is, of course, my husband's favorite.

This is a good example of creating a unique and heartfelt quilt by building a design and color scheme around a simple concept. Sometimes being creative is simply a test in bravery, although love had something to do with it too.

What can you do with a little color knowledge? In this quilt, I used a triple-complement color scheme. I included red and green, violet and gold (yellow), and blue and cheddar (orange). I often tell my classes about the magic of the color cheddar. Cheddar can be either yellow or orange, so you can use it as a complement for both blue and purple. In this quilt, cheddar gives light and life to the whole color scheme. (It also works well with the other complements, red and green.) If you want to work with cheddar in a color scheme, remember that cheddar, like pure yellow, is intense, and you must use it equally in different areas so your eye doesn't stop in one spot.

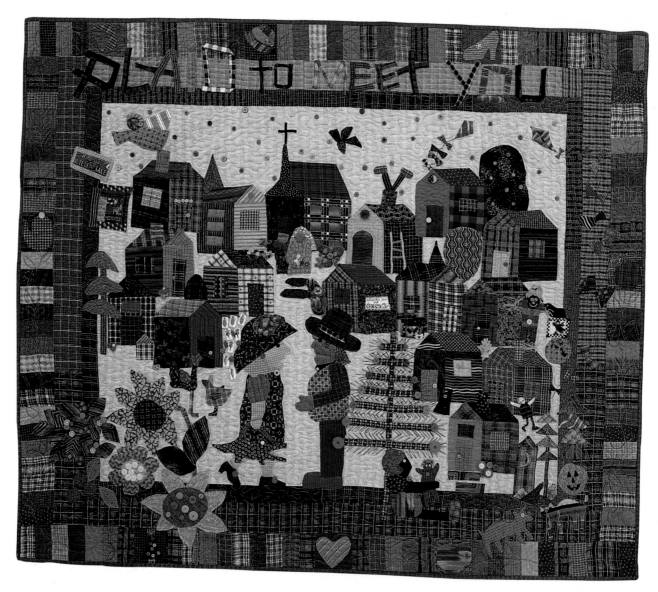

Plaid to Meet You by Mary Lou Weidman, 1993, Spokane, Washington, 72" x 61". Machine quilted by Pam Clarke.

PLAID TO MEET YOU

This quilt was a lot of fun. My theme was plaid fabrics (although I included some graphic prints for variety). I made the pieced houses first, planning to appliqué windows and doors for more variety and color later. Once I positioned the houses, I added my two central figures: a woman and a man. I wanted some whimsy as well, so I gave the woman an alligator bag. I included some of my favorite things: flowers, folk dolls, an angel, a church, and a little humor. (Adding humorous figures and other elements, such as the man falling into the chimney, helps with the chore

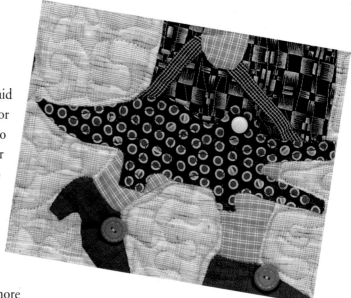

of appliqué. If I can keep a smile going by including something funny, it encourages me.)

I decided to include different seasons for fun: kites, a Christmas feather tree, a garden, quilts on a line, a wedding, and Halloween pumpkins. You may wonder why I would include so many seasons and holidays, but isn't it more creative to include lots of different seasons than to stick with just one? If you don't worry about what people may think, you can do all kinds of fun things to amuse yourself and others.

After quilting, I raided my button stash for flower centers, the sky, and the feather tree. I like to use these plastic treasures liberally.

GOD BLESS US EVERYONE

Christmas has always been a creative time for me, and even though I'm busier then than any other time of year, I like to plan quilts because I feel so creative.

I started this quilt on a trip to see my friend Michelene, who is very creative and also loves Christmas. I chose dark colors, knowing that red and green needed to be included, and cheddar to give light and as a pick-me-up accent. Fabric with lines, stripes, and dots provided personality and added interest.

I strip-pieced the sashing, assembled the background, then began appliquéing the figures. I decided to include our family, so I thought the man and woman should be discussing the tree. (We have a yearly discussion when we choose our tree.) Because my husband always seemed to be holding one of the children and my youngest daughter was always off on her own adventures, I portrayed him holding a child and her feeding a reindeer.

This quilt provided a good place to hang my collection of Christmas pins. Isn't it nice to put these sorts of things where you can see and enjoy them, rather than keeping them in a drawer somewhere? I've been collecting pins and buttons for years, and it was fun to include some on the tree, the angel, and the other blocks.

Think about how you could do an original, creative quilt using the exercises in this book. My students have made delightful Hanukkah hangings for themselves and as gifts for family. These types of quilts are created straight from the heart, which makes them special to see and sew.

For this style of quilt, it's a good idea to piece your background and borders, then appliqué your figures so they cross the sashing pieces and borders (like coloring outside the lines). This nonconformist approach pulls the design together and is more interesting than block after block of figures captured within straight lines.

God Bless Us Everyone
by Mary Lou Weidman, 1994,
Spokane, Washington, 58" x 58".
Machine quilted by Pam Clarke.

Mr. Wonderful Scarecrow by Mary Lou Weidman, 1995, Spokane, Washington, 47" x 56". Machine quilted by Pam Clarke.

MR. WONDERFUL SCARECROW

I love fall, especially fall colors. I wanted a fall quilt that had color, great fabrics, and a little sentiment (and maybe some whimsy). I began by piling up fabrics with "oomph," strong graphics, and color. Scarecrows, birds, and beautiful pumpkins came to mind as I thought about fall. I grabbed my pencil and sketched roughly what I wanted. I try not to draw every little detail or subject because the finished quilts are more appealing if I "go with the flow."

Plus, if I cut as I go, I'm often delightfully surprised.

Once I had a rough idea of what to do with the appliqué, I sewed strips together and picked my background fabrics. This gave me a good sense of the color and where I wanted to position my figures. I cut out Mr. Wonderful and added the supporting characters. After Pam Clarke creatively quilted Mr. Wonderful, I added buttons for color and texture.

IN THE BEGINNING

This was my third Bible-theme quilt. My goal was to convey the story in a folksy, fun design. I wanted to use fabrics that conveyed day and night; earth, sky, and water; and to make a snake you really had to look for. Many people have asked why Adam and Eve aren't wearing fig leaves. At this point in the story, they'd *just* taken a bite of the apple. How would you portray Adam and Eve?

I felt real creative license with this quilt, and I learned a lot about what you can do with a simple idea. Notice the birds' and fishes' expressions? I tried to give them "Oh, no!" looks.

Pam Clarke quilted the "Adam and Eve" into the tree trunk.

In the Beginning
by Mary Lou Weidman, 1993,
Spokane, Washington, 67" x 87".
Machine quilted by Pam Clarke.

Collectibles by Mary Lou Weidman, 1994, Spokane, Washington, 63" x 54". Machine quilted by Pam Clarke.

COLLECTIBLES

I have always loved antiques and collectibles, and I thought this idea would make a creative quilt. I decided to include some of the folksy and whimsical items I look for when I shop. Notice that my doll is holding a cross-stitch sampler in one hand (made by my Aunt Lu) and buttons in the other.

As with all my quilts, fabric and color choices were very important. I chose a light background so the collectibles would show up. For the first border, I used strips of four different patterned fabrics to keep your eye moving around the quilt. I framed the first border with a brightly colored strip-pieced border, then added a black border to push your eye back to the center of the quilt.

As quilters, we collect and admire so many things. When I've used collectibles as a workshop theme, there seems to be no limit to the creative ideas. What collectibles would you choose if you decided to do a little quilt for yourself? Or for someone else? A quilt with this theme makes a nice gift for any collector.

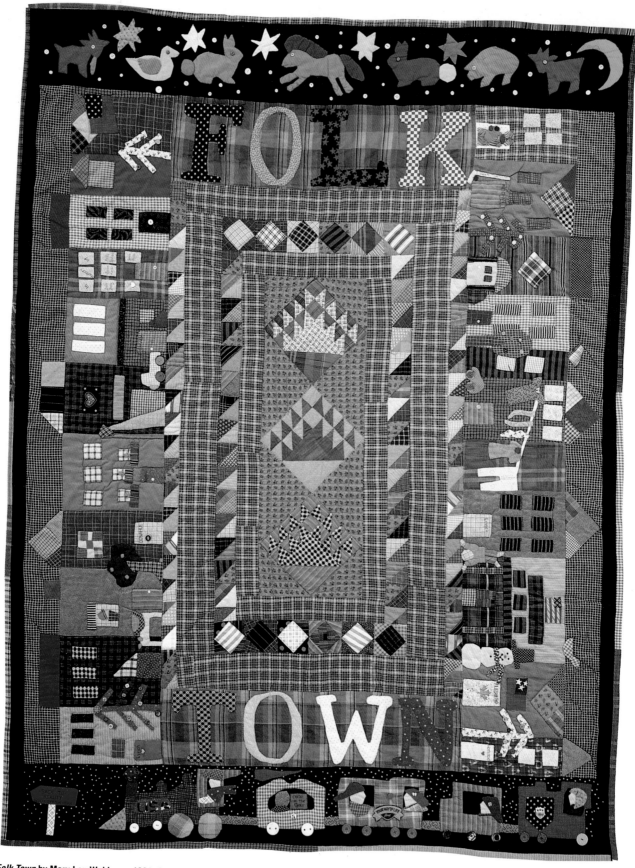

Folk Town **by Mary Lou Weidman, 1991, Spokane, Washington,**
54½" x 54½". Hand quilted.

FOLK TOWN

This is my favorite quilt. It has many memories sewn into it. (It certainly could have been sewn better, but that doesn't matter to me now.) I started with the idea that I wanted to use plaids for a warm and homey feeling. I built a town center with trees (no trunks because this is pretend), then added houses along the sides of the quilt. Each house has either a family name or the name of one of my dearest friends. One house is in memory of quilting friends who have passed away. (Two of those women were my biggest supporters.) My grandmothers' names are on the door of this house.

My daughter's boyfriend asked me to include his white truck that year. He was disappointed with how I portrayed it, not knowing the concept of folk art, I guess. I added folk and baby dolls at the top (I collect these) and a hockey stick with the names of two boys that lived with our family that year.

The only person in the neighborhood is a little boy who's standing on his head. This represents the years our son had cancer and how it turned our lives upside down.

The seasons are represented by Christmas trees, a watermelon, and other signs of different seasons. The sky is happy with varied folk figures.

The train at the bottom holds family members. My husband is the engineer. I am in the next car, portrayed as watching television because I watched the Gulf crisis

nightly as I worked on this quilt. The next car has my son and his red-headed girlfriend. The last two cars carry my two daughters. The road sign says, "Back to Reality Avenue" because I knew that when I finished, it would be time to face the things we must all do.

I included a Bible verse on the back of this quilt. If you have a favorite poem, verse, or wise and wonderful saying, share it with future generations by writing it on your quilts. I know that someday, someone will read what I've written, and I want to offer wisdom and comfort to that person.

Mrs. Donahue Meets Mrs. Flesberg by Mary Lou Weidman, 1991, Spokane, Washington, 35" x 35". Machine quilted by Gayle Snitselaar.

MRS. DONAHUE MEETS MRS. FLESBERG

This quilt began with a group of fabrics used in a manufacturer's challenge for Quilt Market. Looking at them, I thought of my grandmothers' jersey dresses. I also realized that I had to use only the fabrics given, which meant that my grandmothers would have to be either purple or green. Fortunately, I happen to think purple and green people is a great idea. My grandmothers became green and, really, no one has commented on that. What people do notice is that my grandmothers have rather large noses. That's okay; it makes them more interesting.

I think this quilt captures the essence of both women. Grandma Donahue loved flashy jewelry and was very nurturing. Grandma Flesberg was very sweet and loved giving tea parties. The jewelry, watch, and buttons on this quilt belonged to both my grandmothers, making it even more special.

COOPER KITTY

My daughter Shari moved to New Brunswick, Canada, when she got married. New Brunswick is a long way from Spokane, Washington. To ease her homesickness, she bought a little calico cat and named him "Cooper," after a brand of hockey equipment. (Her husband is a goaltender.)

Shari and I talked weekly about who was doing what at home and what quilt I was working on. I knew she would be pleased to learn that I was working on a Cooper Kitty quilt.

The graphic, yarnlike fabrics made a great ball and border. Pam Clarke quilted balls of yarn in the border for playful color and texture.

Shari told me that the neighbor children giggled when they saw Cooper Kitty. There is no better compliment.

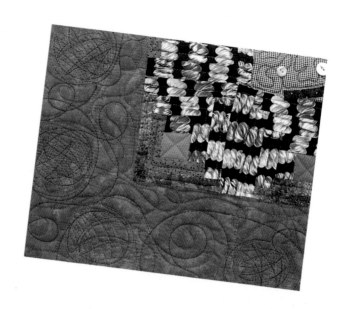

Cooper Kitty by Mary Lou Weidman, 1995, Spokane, Washington, 40" x 60½". Machine quilted by Pam Clarke.

Folk Ark by Mary Lou Weidman, 1990, Spokane, Washington,
76" x 89½". Hand quilted.

FOLK ARK

After reading an article describing the many different cultures with stories about an ark, I decided to create a folk ark. At first, I planned to have Mrs. Noah sweeping on the deck, but in the end I went with an in-charge-looking Mr. Noah and whimsical animals.

To communicate the idea and theme, I paraphrased three Bible verses in the border. I added "In a calm storm, every man is pilot" as a truism for my children. This is one of their favorite quilts.

As you can see, I sewed lots and lots of bugle beads around the ark. I think the best thing about this quilt is that when it's hanging, all those beads shimmer as if it were raining.

I feel now that I could have gone farther creatively with this idea. I think I'll do more with it some day.

Five Easy Pieces by Mary Lou Weidman, 1993, Spokane, Washington, 54½" x 61½". Machine quilted by Pam Clarke.

FIVE EASY PIECES

This quilt is about things I love. The first row has blue dishes of all kinds. The second row has all kinds of hats. The third row has folk dolls, which I adore. The fourth row has fattening foods, which I wish I weren't so fond of. (I'm sure I inherited my passion for pie from my paternal grandmother.) The fifth row has folk figures, including a man with a fish and a fry pan. Interestingly enough, most people think the fisherman is holding a cleaver. That's OK; they're being creative too.

Although there are many different fabrics and colors in this quilt, it works because I used a color formula (see page 65). If you analyze how I used color, you'll see that I consistently mixed complementary colors in the rows and borders. For the outside border, I chose red and green for the dominant colors and mixed these with the fabrics used in the rows and sashing strips. Because I used a color formula, it works well.

SIX OF ONE, A HALF DOZEN OF MY MOTHER

I love language and using words to help me stretch when creating quilts. You can see that I used the number 1 in six different ways. I also portrayed my mother in six different ways. She's reading the Bible, gardening, serving a sick child soda and gingerbread cookies, exercising, sitting with grandchildren on a sofa, and, finally, holding me as a child (in the photo). Use simple ideas that are sentimental and dear to you to create a one-of-a-kind quilt.

Six of One, a Half Dozen of My Mother by Mary Lou Weidman, 1994, Spokane, Washington, 66½" x 50". Machine quilted by Dana Pendergrath.

Too Hot by Mary Lou Weidman, 1994, Spokane, Washington, 43½" x 52". Machine quilted by Barb Durheim.

TOO HOT

This quilt is the result of a Neighborhood Challenge class. I'd made several neighborhood quilts as class samples, and I was ready to do one with a different twist.

While one of my kids was on a date, I started thinking about a place where kids "parked" when I was young. It had a wonderful view of the houses in the valley below and the stars above. Before I knew it, I had a couple in a car, an owl with button eyes, wildly colored houses in the valley, and a great moon.

The title "Too Hot" became the license plate, and the lime green buttons became the stars. The striped border fabric and lime green buttons were perfect for this intense color scheme.

PLAID PARK

I love to people-watch. So, after a summer traveling, I created a park featuring some of the people I'd seen. My park includes people from Southern California, Phoenix, and Seattle as well as the Calgary Stampede in Canada. No kidding. I couldn't have made up these people.

When I started this quilt, I told myself "Only plaids." I worked on blending memorable personalities, fun shapes, bright colors, and little details to create an amusing quilt to remember the year by. And, of course, I added embellishments to make it more enjoyable.

Plaid Park by Mary Lou Weidman, 1995, Spokane, Washington, 72" x 95". Machine quilted by Pam Clarke.

TIME TO SAY "I LOVE YOU"

One day, when my daughter was leaving with friends for a dance, I called "I love you." She replied, "I don't have time!" I ran to the entry, playfully grabbed her, kissed her, and said, "There's always time to say I love you!"

That night, I started this quilt. The family is cheddar colored because I'm sure that any family lucky enough to be this color has to be very happy. I added watches, the family dog, my two girls, and my son. Everyone is smiling.

The pieced heart in the center adds color and interest to the design. The numbers *24* and *7* stand for my youngest daughter's pet phrase that year: "24 hours a day, 7 days a week."

I used my family to portray the most important idea in this quilt—everyone is reaching out to another.

Time to Say "I Love You" by Mary Lou Weidman, 1994, Spokane, Washington, 90½" x 97½". Machine quilted by Pam Clarke.

Java Dreams by Mary Lou Weidman, 1995, Spokane, Washington, 59" x 59". Machine quilted by Pam Clarke.

JAVA DREAMS

We have truly wonderful coffees and espressos in the Northwest (maybe it's the weather), and I love starting my day with a latté. So much so, in fact, that I've earned the nickname "latté girl" from friends.

One night, I had a funny dream about coffee cups and lattés. Because I couldn't remember the details, I decided to imagine my own java dreams. A man and a woman in their nightclothes float through dreamland. A sleepy sun rises to greet another day. Coffee cups march forward to greet thirsty customers.

When it came to quilting, Pam Clarke liberally machine quilted coffee cups and coffee-company names for fun. After Pam finished the quilting, I lavishly embellished the quilt with sequins, pins, and what-have-yous.

Wouldn't this be fun in a coffee shop or as a gift for another coffee addict? How would you use this theme?

Tea for Two by Mary Lou Weidman, 1994, Spokane, Washington,
59" x 50½". Machine quilted by Gayle Snitselaar.

TEA FOR TWO

Memories are my best inspiration. This quilt began with memories of my grandmother's tea parties and an old tea towel. What did I remember best about my grandmother's tea parties? There were always lots of homemade goodies. Also, grandmother liked teapots, old photos, hats, cats, purses, flowers, and jewelry. So, how could I include all these ideas?

I used the tea towel as a tablecloth. It was fun to think of ways I could make tea cakes and jelly cookies. (Old celluloid buttons became perfect candies.) All the photos on the wall were special to my grandmother.

Incorporating these pieces of the past make this memory quilt special and something I can share with my children and friends.

JUST COLOR ME RED, WHITE, AND BLUE

This quilt is a little piece of history. As the crisis unfolded in Kuwait, my neighbor, who lost her husband in the Vietnam War, came over to watch television with me. As we listened to the latest reports, she turned to me and, with tears in her eyes, said, "Just color me red, white, and blue."

I started the quilt that night, without a design in mind, and let it happen. Over time, I've added old pins and buttons found in my travels. Like the pins and buttons, that war is now part of the past.

Just Color Me Red, White, and Blue by Mary Lou Weidman, 1990, Spokane, Washington, 51½" x 60". Machine quilted by Pam Clarke.

Simply Folk by Mary Lou Weidman, 1993, Spokane, Washington, 49" x 55". Hand quilted.

SIMPLY FOLK

This quilt began what I call my "dating series." When my older daughter started to date, I would stay up and work on a quilt until she got home. (I got a lot of quilts done that way.)

I collected folk dolls, and I wanted a quilt as a backdrop for my dolls. This gave me a chance to use a subject and fabrics I loved. I experimented with color and value, as well as with tying a quilt instead of quilting it. The buttons add to the folksy look of this quilt, providing color and texture.

This quilt is another favorite because every time I see it, I remember family events and friends I had. My dating series continued through three children. Not many people understood my approach to creativity in those days, but I was happy and quite content in what I was doing.

ROOSTER IN THE HEN HOUSE

I like to piece quilt backgrounds (with no plan for the theme or characters), then set them aside until a creative idea strikes. I sometimes make several backgrounds in the course of a week. This is how "Rooster in the Hen House" began. My friend Shauna saw this background lying on my studio floor and said, "Hey, how about rooster in the hen house?" After she left, I dashed to the fabric cupboard and pulled together a pile of fabrics compatible with the background. I ended up with a rooster, two hens, and a newly hatched chick—another "it-just-happened" quilt.

Rooster in the Hen House by Mary Lou Weidman, 1995, Spokane, Washington, 56" x 45". Machine quilted by Pam Clarke.

THE RUMMAGE SALE

I love to create quilts about people and things and hobbies I love, and I love rummage sales! Years ago, I saw two women get into a tug-of-war over an old quilt. If I hadn't had two children in tow, I might have joined the tug-of-war myself. I made sure my quilt included things I would like to find. I also included a photo of my grandmother and great uncle, a little thing to make this quilt more personal.

The Rummage Sale by Mary Lou Weidman, 1993, Spokane, Washington, 53½" x 44½". Machine quilted by Gayle Snitselaar.

Manito Park by Mary Lou Weidman, 1994, Spokane, Washington, 51" x 58". Machine quilted by Pam Clarke.

MANITO PARK

A trip to this park, my favorite in our hometown, is a sign that summer has arrived. As with many of my quilts, I included family members. My husband likes to garden and is often hauling something in a wheelbarrow. The year I made this, my son was interested in surfing, and my younger daughter was involved in track and running. My older daughter is walking toward the buildings. The family dog is there, and my Aunt Bess's name is on one of the antique-shop windows.

Ted and Geneva Dance the Light Fantastic by Mary Lou Weidman, 1993, Spokane, Washington, 42" x 54". Machine quilted by Gayle Snitselaar.

TED AND GENEVA DANCE THE LIGHT FANTASTIC

Several years ago, I received an offer to make a number of quilts for a group of restaurants. I thought a series of dance quilts would be fun, with a different dance in each for variety. When I was small, I loved to watch my parents dance around the living room; they're the inspiration for this quilt.

After I finished it, I remembered a marvelous story. My friend Molly and her husband were going to an elegant dance in a grand hotel. In anticipation, Molly bought an expensive gown with a wonderful, billowy skirt. The night of the dance arrived, and Molly and her husband felt fabulous. As they danced, Molly noticed that all eyes were upon her, and she danced as she had never danced before. Toward the end of the dance, Molly moved her hand to the back of her dress and discovered that her wonderful, billowy skirt was tucked into her girdle. This is a story and theme we can all relate to!

WEIDMAN SNOW FAMILY

While working on an idea for a class, I thought, "Who doesn't love the image of happy snowmen?" Anyone can make snowmen, but why not depict your family as snow people? I used hats, scarves, body positions, facial expressions, and vintage buttons to give each family member/ snow person a different look. My son-in-law is represented by the snowman button in one of the house windows.

Some of my students added snow dogs and cats to their snow families. How about a snow horse or farm animal? You could have a lot of fun with this idea.

Weidman Snow Family by Mary Lou Weidman, 1995, Spokane, Washington, 48" x 42". Machine quilted by Pam Clarke.

Folk and Fleurs by Mary Lou Weidman, 1995, Spokane, Washington, 58" x 67". Machine quilted by Pam Clarke.

FOLK AND FLEURS

This quilt is the result of one of my classes, aptly titled "Container Quilts." I wanted to make something that looked like a folksy Victorian basket. As usual, I chose to fill my basket with things I love: a big bunny, an angel, flowers, a flag, a doll, lots of vintage buttons, and so on.

This quilt looks good anywhere and always draws people who want to see how many things they can recognize. I plan to do lots more of these!

COWPOKE FOLK

This quilt is, of course, a play on words. I wanted to make a folk-style quilt with lots of whimsical cowpoke characters. As I often do, I fabricated this story around my family. That's me with the lasso, pulling my husband off of his horse. The signpost points to three mountains named after my children.

To enhance the mood, I added longhorn steers, an iguana, and a chicken. The borders explain the theme.

Notice how I used plaids cut off grain to add movement and excitement. Use this trick to pull the viewer's eye to different areas in your quilt.

Cowpoke Folk by Mary Lou Weidman, 1990, Spokane, Washington, 68½" x 82". Machine quilted by Gayle Snitselaar.

Tribute to Peppers by Mary Lou Weidman, 1990, Spokane, Washington, 70" x 80". Machine quilted by Gayle Snitselaar.

TRIBUTE TO PEPPERS

While visiting Phoenix, I fell in love with the extraordinary colors in the scenery, clothing, and buildings I saw there. In a local quilt shop, I found pepper-patterned fabric that I knew would be perfect in a Phoenix quilt.

One of my favorite parts of our trip was the glorious hot, spicy food we ate at Mexican restaurants. I ate so much that I had heartburn for a week after I returned home. Hot, hot, hot peppers seemed a fitting theme, with a little humor thrown in. No matter what the style of quilt, you can always throw in a little humor.

ANIMAL STACK

I've started making animal-theme quilts, and I love how creative I can be with this idea. "Animal Stack" is another just-let-it-happen quilt. I mixed bright colors and humor in a quilt that would be perfect for a child's room or anywhere you wanted something to make you smile. Think about what kind of folk animals you'd stack to make someone smile.

Animal Stack by Mary Lou Weidman, 1996, Spokane, Washington, 43½" x 61". Machine quilted by Pam Clarke.

Country Still Life by Mary Lou Weidman, 1995, Spokane, Washington, 49" x 52". Machine quilted by Pam Clarke.

COUNTRY STILL LIFE

This quilt hangs in my family room. The cheddar-colored background, my favorite, invited color play. (Cheddar makes almost any color come alive.) Because I love the look of plaids cut off grain, I cut the border fabric off grain. I used complementary colors for the figures. Note that the rooster is only a simple silhouette. Simple shapes can be very interesting and are often more successful than complex shapes in this style of quilt.

AUDUBON ANGEL

When he was eight years old, my son asked "Do animals have guardian angels, Mom?" I don't remember my answer, but the question inspired this lively quilt about an off-kilter angel who loves birds. The bird and angel fabrics were inspiring. The solids and graphic black-and-white fabrics make a powerful border.

Audubon Angel by Mary Lou Weidman, 1996, Spokane, Washington, 42" x 40½". Machine quilted by Pam Clarke.

Animal Crackers by Mary Lou Weidman, 1995, Spokane, Washington, 55" x 68". Machine quilted by Pam Clarke.

ANIMAL CRACKERS

In one of my classes, I teach students a little bit about color and how to make spontaneous-looking animals. At the end of class, each student trades an animal for one made by another student. I created this quilt from the animals I received. Pam Clarke machine quilted cookie-cutter animals in the cheddar-colored borders.

Children love this quilt. Perhaps this theme would be a nice way to stretch your creative quotient. Try making a personalized version of "Animal Crackers" for someone young. All you have to do is say "I'm going to do it." And you will.

LET US GIVE THANKS

This is a perfect theme for a creative quilt. I used complementary colors in the Nine Patch borders and in the appliquéd figures for a folksy, primitive look. Buttons added color and texture.

This is a good quilt to hang up at Thanksgiving, but it's nice to remember to be thankful all year long.

Let Us Give Thanks by Mary Lou Weidman, 1990, Spokane, Washington, 60" x 60". Machine quilted by Pam Clarke.

THREADBARE

For many years, my family hosted foreign-exchange students. In fact, we hosted more than fifty students from four different countries in sixteen years. To people who are just learning our language, words and phrases we take for granted often don't make sense. One young Japanese woman pointed out that I said "Oh, brother!" a lot. I soon tried to work that phrase out of my vocabulary so I wouldn't have to explain what it meant.

I kept a list of ambiguous words and phrases, and one day, it dawned on me to use these as inspiration for quilt designs. "Threadbare" is one result.

Threadbare by Mary Lou Weidman, 1995, Spokane, Washington, 37" x 33½". Machine quilted by Pam Clarke.

HEN PARTY

"Hen Party" was inspired by a friend's move to Montana. I designed a simple Chicken block pattern in honor of Becky, who loves chickens, and passed it to members of the Magpies, my quilt group. We made a friendship quilt from the blocks, hoping that Becky would remember our hen parties.

Hen Party, blocks by (left to right) Debbie Hodin, Linda Sullivan, Carol Campbell, Pam Clarke, Nancy Goodyear, Shauna Stewart, Manda Benton, Linda Roedl, Chris Bristow, Lori Aluna, Mary Lou Weidman, Bev Freeman, Barb Durheim, Jackie Wolff, Manya Powell, and Julie Lynch, 1995, Spokane, Washington, 76" x 76". Assembled by Manya Powell. Machine quilted by Pam Clarke.

HEN PARTY– GONE WILD

After the original quilt went to Montana, I went to my fabric stash and pulled wild colors and fun prints for another, wilder hen party. I added sashing to the blocks, then cut them off-kilter for a folksy, whimsical look. This quilt makes people of all ages smile. If you'd like to try it, the applique pattern is on page 89.

Hen Party–Gone Wild by Mary Lou Weidman, 1995, Spokane, Washington, 52" x 51½". Machine quilted by Pam Clarke.

THOSE THREE BEARS

I have always loved the story of the three bears. When my children were small, I would change the details of the story from time to time to see if they were listening.

I wanted to make some fun quilts with fairy-tale themes, so I decided to portray the three bears with my older daughter as Goldilocks. (She's blonde.) As usual, I didn't worry about skin color.

To add interest, I embellished this quilt with bits of history. Papa bear is wearing a World War I medal my son-in-law's grandfather won. The buttons on his vest include two from the artillery division of the Royal Canadian Air Force, two from the American Air Force, one from the Soviet military, one from a cavalry division of the Royal Canadian Mounted Police, and one from a firefighter's uniform. What bits of history can you add to your quilts?

Those Three Bears by Mary Lou Weidman, 1996, Spokane, Washington, 59" x 52½". Machine quilted by Pam Clarke.

Cajun Katy Loves Bayou Bob by Mary Lou Weidman, 1995, Spokane, Washington, 36" x 45". Hand quilted.

CAJUN KATY LOVES BAYOU BOB

This quilt began with the idea of using bright colors and cyanotype (sun-reactive) fabric with word play (see page 72). I featured a folksy couple, an alligator, a parrot, and a snake. A pair of my daughter's old snake earrings were perfect for Cajun Katy. This is a stretch-your-imagination project.

SANTA AND ME IN '53

I remember having this picture taken with Santa. I was scared to death. My mother paid to have a recording of me talking to Santa, but I wasn't about to talk to that strange man. Mother was not very happy with her recording of dead silence. I can laugh about this story now, so I included the photo and other holiday symbols in a special Christmas quilt. Seasonal or holiday quilts are great ways to channel your creativity. If you have a favorite holiday, why not work it into a new project?

Santa and Me in '53 by Mary Lou Weidman, 1995, Spokane, Washington, 41½" x 41½". Machine quilted by Pam Clarke.

When Pigs Fly by Mary Lou Weidman, 1993, Spokane, Washington, 52" x 62". Machine quilted by Gayle Snitselaar.

WHEN PIGS FLY

This was my first attempt at stenciling (see page 72). I used this approach for the letters and stars, and along the way, I learned a lot about textile paint and freezer paper.

My plan was to start with simple fabrics and add interest through the story, characters, and embellishments. I included a marquee with Elvis for laughs, a theater featuring C. S. Lewis's *The Great Divorce,* and a restaurant owned by two dear friends.

I found wooden buttons for the pig snouts while traveling. They were meant for sweaters and woolens. The friendly clerk asked, "What are you going to do with these nice buttons?" When I replied, "Oh, I'm going to use them as pig snouts on a quilt," she handed me the sack and promptly left. What can I say?

DON'T LET THE LITTLE THINGS BUG YOU

We often let things that don't matter get the best of us. My mother says, "In a hundred years, what will it matter?" I wanted to make a quilt with this theme, so I decided to make a woman surrounded by folksy bugs.

In the quilting, Pam Clarke included some of the little things that bugged us in the quilting, such as bills, slow traffic, gray hair, and deadlines.

Don't Let the Little Things Bug You by Mary Lou Weidman, 1996, Spokane, Washington, 52" x 52". Machine quilted by Pam Clarke.

Friends from Afar by Mary Lou Weidman, 1993, Spokane, Washington, 34" x 34". Machine quilted by Gayle Snitselaar.

FRIENDS FROM AFAR

For this quilt, I began with the idea of making up a story centered around my three children and other things I love, such as the little folk-style quilt and doll, a photo of my kids and two boys that lived with us that year, a baseball (my son played that year), a tea set, plenty of buttons, and a spider for luck. I used rubber stamps to tell the story around the figures. This quilt, with its sentiment and humor, is one of my favorites.

A Short Story by Mary Lou Weidman
Before bedtime, in twilight hours, Mama reads to her sweeties from the book Friends from Afar. Just then, as if by magic, an alien from the planet Zanthar appears to bring friendly greetings and to hopefully receive a dinner invitation someday soon. The End

PART FOUR

QUILT RECIPES

How do you take a theme or story, make it grow, and then turn it into a quilt? It's as easy as writing an English paper (depending on your teacher, of course). This section provides simple guidelines you can follow to make your quilts and stories more appealing and unique.

But before you begin, I have a secret to share with you. There are two enemies of action: fear and lack of confidence. These feelings are common. If I asked a roomful of quilters, "Are there any artists in this group?" very few would raise their hands. If I asked a roomful of first-graders the same question, very few *wouldn't* raise their hands.

As a teacher, I've found that everyone has the ability to use their creativity and individual style to make marvelous quilts. The secret is to give yourself permission to be creative. As soon as you give yourself permission to make a creative quilt, new ideas will start popping into your head. Before you know it, you'll be wondering if you'll have enough time to use all your great ideas!

Developing a Theme

People often ask me if everything reminds me of a quilt theme. Actually, I trained myself to think this way, and it's become a habit. The nice thing about this habit is that I have more ideas than I'll get to in my lifetime. I want to do stories about the lady at the supermarket who looked tired and crabby, a child's first day at school, my friend's new dance lessons, my dad's booming vegetable garden, and the pan of cookies I burned the other day. Even simple, everyday events could be charming quilts. Over time, these become a diary of your life.

By now, you may have so many theme ideas that you don't know where to start. Pick a quiet place without distractions, then choose one of your themes or one listed below and brainstorm ideas to support your theme. Keep a notebook handy to jot down thoughts that come to you. The ideas I have for these words vary from day to day, so doing this exercise at different times, days, and even seasons will bring you different ideas and results.

airplanes	cold things
America	collections
art	dancing
astronomy	danger
autos, trucks, engines	eating
barnyard	eggs
bubble bath	elves
beaches	embarrassing things
beggars	fashions
being alone	fishing
buildings	food
busy people	future
camping	games
carnivals 'n' fairs	gifts
childhood	habits
china	jobs

COLLECTIONS

"What lies behind us and what lies before us are tiny matters, compared to what lies within us."

RALPH WALDO EMERSON

kisses
lake cabins
luck
neighbors
new baby
parades
pastimes
rabbits
rain
scary things
school

telephone talk
time flies
tiny things
toys
tree houses
trips to the dentist
way out West
wild things

Using Quilters' Clues

Quilters' clues—visual hints—are one of the most important and often overlooked aspects of storytelling in quilts. We want to know why a subject was important to you so we can really enjoy the thought behind it.

Quilters' clues include seasons, time (clocks), printed signs, stages of life, the way someone looks, the neighborhood they lived in, and almost anything that goes with the theme. For example, if you are doing a quilt about the chili cook-off you attended in Texas, think of clues to help us see, taste, and feel what the cook-off was like. A bowl of chili sitting on a quilt isn't going to do much (and would probably look strange), but a big sign that says "Chili Cook-Off" over a bowl of chili speaks volumes. If you add a cowboy with fire shooting out of his ears and tears falling from his eyes and a border with red chili peppers, we'll think your quilt is creative as well as interesting.

Whatever your theme or central character, try to think of ideas to support it. What is your central character doing and where? What do you want us to know about your central character? What is important for you to say about this person, place, or thing? Like reading a novel, it's the supporting cast and background detail that draw us in.

Think of easy and functional ideas; you don't have to appliqué or piece everything. Fabric can help, as well as embellishments. For example, how would you show us that your grandmother liked cats, cherry pies, and bingo? Cherry pie and cat print fabrics might do the trick (although a kitty pattern might be more interesting). You might piece, machine embroider, or use Pigma™ pens to paint a bingo board on your quilt. How about using buttons for bingo markers or cherries? I like to include names and maybe a little information. Perhaps you could include your grandmother's name or the words "I love my grandma." Finally, don't forget to include personal things—Grandma's old buttons, jewelry, or dress fabric. These quilts become treasures for not only you but for everyone who knew and loved your grandmother.

If you have a good variety of quilters' clues, you will have a fun, unique, and successful quilt. Just make sure the clues are prominent enough for us to see them.

"Conform and be dull."

J. FRANK DOBIE

Whatever Happened to the Little Girl from Brown's Addition?
by Mary Lou Weidman, 1993, Spokane, Washington,
56" x 58". Machine quilted by Gayle Snitselaar.

WHATEVER HAPPENED TO THE LITTLE GIRL FROM BROWN'S ADDITION?

This quilt is a great example of developing a theme and providing quilters' clues. To start, I thought back to my childhood. We lived in a wonderful neighborhood called "Brown's Addition," and I wanted to use this for my theme. Next, I made a list of ideas and things—quilters' clues—I could use to support my theme. At right is the planning sheet from my notebook.

After I made up this list, I got my fabric together and started on my quilt. Because I wanted people to know that this took place in Brown's Addition, I made a sign that was large enough to notice. To make it fun and more interesting, I included vines and a spider and web.

- Title: "Whatever Happened to the Little Girl from Brown's Addition?"

- A house with large trees and lots of flowers

- An old car with large headlights and a cat named Whiskers

- I had braids when I lived there.

- A hollyhock bush with beautiful summer blooms and seedpods we played with later

- I have photos of me, my parents, and my grandmother taken in Brown's Addition. I could use these photos in the windows and doorway.

- It would be fun to include a woman (me) looking back and saying, "What happened to that little girl, and where has the time gone?"

- Include old buttons and handmade linens that our neighbor, Maxine Gaetano, gave me. Maybe I could put the buttons on the lady's hat and use the old linens for the quilt backing.

- I have an old hankie and belt buckle that belonged to my grandmother. I could include it for luck and love. Maybe I could tuck the hankie into the lady's blouse.

I used handmade linens to embellish the back of *Whatever Happened to the Little Girl from Brown's Addition?*

Creating Eye-Catching Quilts

Now that you have a theme and lots of ideas and quilters' clues to support it, how do you use these to create an eye-catching quilt? Try the following creative options, which invite the viewer's eye.

- Exaggerate
- Give movement
- Simplify
- Use the borders
- Repeat, repeat, repeat

Exaggerate

When you draw people, animals, or things in your quilts, exaggerate some part of the figure (hair, hands, noses, tails, legs, etc.). When I made "Mrs. Donahue Meets Mrs. Flesberg" (page 26), I exaggerated my grandmothers' noses and hands. Also, I put a huge ring on one of the hands. Think about a caricature; exaggerating makes the figure more fun and interesting.

Give Movement

Portray your figures running, throwing, jumping, walking, bending, hugging, or falling down a chimney as in "Plaid to Meet You" (page 18). Moving figures tell the story, and they are much more involving.

Simplify

Simplify, simplify, simplify. Quilters often believe that figures have to be perfect, with precise shadows and details. This is not necessary. Use simple shapes to tell your story. When you look at children's drawings, you'll notice that they focus on what the people are doing rather than what they look like. Keep in mind that a dog can be made from a rounded rectangle with stick legs. The viewer is usually more interested in what your dog is doing or how it ties into the story than whether the dog looks simple or weird. If the viewer is more interested in picking apart your figures, then they're missing the point. (You do want to complete this quilt in your lifetime, don't you?)

Use the Borders

Rather than using borders to close in your story, make them part of the story. Add figures to support your theme. If you are telling a story about springtime, think about including May baskets, tulips, sunshine, lilies, hats, or bunnies in your borders. For example, look at "Folk Ark" (page 28). The animals and words in my borders are an essential part of the story and quilt design.

Repeat, Repeat, Repeat

Repeating different figures is fun and an easy way to use creativity in quilting. For example, look at "Five Easy Pieces" (page 30). What if you repeated a person over and over in different fabrics? How about repeating cats or stars or hearts? The possibilities are unlimited.

"Variety of mere nothings gives more pleasure than uniformity of something."

JEAN PAUL RICHTER

Choosing Colors and Fabrics

I'm often asked how I choose fabric for a quilt. Many people look at the number of fabrics I use in a quilt and assume I just grab whatever is handy. No so.

When I decide to start a new project, I go to my fabric stash and choose one color of fabric. Everything that follows is based on that choice. Next, I pick a complementary color and one other color, either a primary or secondary color. I choose my fabric and build my color scheme around these three colors. This formula always works well. Simply pick colors within the three color families and have fun.

Thinking about color is as important as seeing color. Do you need a change and want to try a simple new approach to color? Try an analogous or complementary color scheme. Adding colors and complements is more complicated than the basic formula discussed above, but you can get sensational results.

For an analogous color scheme, choose three or four colors that are next to each other on the color wheel. For more interest, add a small amount of one complement.

Combine these with a neutral background or black for a creative color scheme.

For a complementary color scheme, choose two complements and use them in different amounts. Combine these with other complements, neutrals, or black.

Color Keys

I've been teaching a color class for years. I always begin the class by asking each student for their favorite color, their least favorite color, and their biggest color problem. I've learned that quilters, no matter where they live, have similar likes, dislikes, and problems. I suppose this phenomenon may be related to advertising, clothing, and home-decorating trends.

Jewel tones are the favorites. Most quilters like blue, purple, and green and dislike orange and bright yellow. I suspect this is because orange and yellow are intense colors and can be hard to work with. And, at the moment, orange is not a popular color for home decorating.

The biggest problem is a color that looks great on the bolt, but not in the quilt. Study the color wheel and color relationships described below so you understand how colors work together, then try the following tricks.

❤ Are you using too much of a good thing? Watch out for complementary colors. Fabric designers know it is visually appealing to include different amounts of complementary colors. But, when we look at equal or nearly equal amounts of complementary colors, we see warm gray or brown. If you place equal or nearly equal amounts of two complements next to each other on a background, they may gray the background color.

❤ Can you see how the color and lines in the fabric will look when cut up? Make a viewing template. Take a piece of white tagboard or typing paper and cut a 6" x 6" square. Cut a 3" x 4" rectangle from the center of the square. Take this template to the fabric store and use it to look at those bolts you aren't sure about. Try rotating the template. This could change your buying habits and your quilts.

❤ Is it too loud, or not loud enough? I avoid fabrics that have lots of white. They often don't mix well with other fabrics. I also avoid intense yellow, hot pink, pure red, eye-popping blue, and brilliant green. However, everyone has different tastes. What I consider to be tasteful and pretty, my students may consider loud and obnoxious.

Most quilters feel one of two ways about color. They are either interested in learning more about it, or they are afraid of it. There are many good books about color on the market, and I encourage you to spend some time researching color. I am including some basics to help make this sometimes threatening task easier.

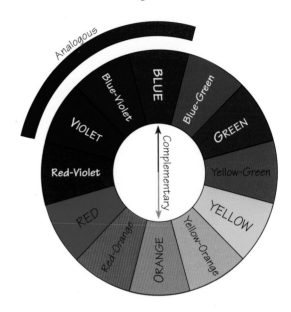

Hue or polychromatic: Other terms for color.

Tint: A tint is made by taking any color and adding white. Pastels are tints.

Shade: A shade is made by taking any color and adding black. Many fabrics are printed with black over a color to make a shade.

Tone: A tone is made by taking any color and adding gray or brown. Many country-style fabrics are tones.

Value: Value is the lightness or darkness of a color. Dull quilts have only one value—either light, medium, or dark. I find that we all tend to favor a certain value. I love dark fabrics, and I have to make an effort to buy those badly needed light and medium fabrics. Many of my students love pastels and are afraid of darker shades. A creative quilter knows she has to jumble these values together for success.

Intensity: Intense colors are pure, without white, gray, or black. The purer the color, the brighter or more intense the fabric. Your eye is attracted by intense colors. When you work with intense fabrics, remember to move the color across the face of the quilt.

Primary colors: Red, blue, and yellow are the three primary colors. These are the colors from which all others are mixed.

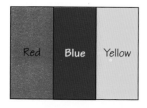

Primary Colors

Secondary colors: Green, purple, and orange are secondary colors, a mix of two primary colors.

Secondary Colors

Tertiary colors: Red-orange, blue-green, and blue-violet are tertiary colors, a mix of a primary and secondary color. I call these "in-between" colors.

Tertiary Colors

Warm colors: Red, orange, and yellow are warm colors. When you use these colors in a design with cool colors, they appear to advance. Warm colors feel exciting, vibrant, and emotionally charged. Think of a hot burner on a stove, a crackling fire, and sunshine.

Cool colors: Blue, green, and purple are cool colors. When you use these colors in a design with warm colors, they appear to retreat. Cool colors feel restful and refreshing. Think of water, trees, distant mountains, and snow.

Monochromatic color scheme: Using one color and its tints, shades, and tones.

Monochromatic
Color Scheme

Analogous color scheme: Using three colors that are adjacent to each other on the color wheel, such as blue, blue-violet, and violet.

Analogous
Color Scheme

Complementary color scheme: Using colors that are opposite each other on the color wheel, such as blue and orange. Artists learn that using different amounts of complementary colors enhance color schemes.

Complementary
Color Scheme

Fabric Personalities

Your fabric choices are as important as your color choices. Fabric that looks great on the bolt doesn't always look great when you get it home. The following tips can help you choose the fabrics for your creative quilts.

❤ To make scrappy quilts, you need lots of variety. But this doesn't mean you need yards and yards of fabric. I buy lots of ¼- and ⅓-yard pieces. This provides plenty of variety and enough fabric for my scrappy quilts.

❤ To pull the different fabrics together, I buy 1½ yards of a simple print, plaid, or tone-on-tone for my background. Try to find a print that reads as a solid from a distance. Choose a fabric with a simple color scheme: black with a small beige print or washed-out gold plaid. The background helps pull together the many different colors and patterns.

❤ The scale of the prints in your quilt is important. When you shop for fabrics, make sure you include small, medium, and large prints. If all your prints are tiny, your quilt will appear boring. On the other hand, if all your prints are large, your quilt will look overdone. Mix different-scale prints to make your quilt visually appealing.

How we see a color is related to the other colors near or around it. To choose colors for your quilt, you need to understand the basics of the color wheel and the relationships. I recommend memorizing the primary and secondary colors. When you select fabric, group tertiary colors in a primary or secondary category. This approach makes it easier to analyze color schemes. For example, if your fabric is blue-violet and you categorize it as blue, it's easy to determine the complementary color—orange or cheddar.

❤ Texture is another consideration. Textured fabrics look furry, nubby, lumpy, woven, velvety, and so on. The contrast in these fabrics provides dimension and depth.

Don't forget to work out your color formula before you choose your fabrics. With the color formula and great fabrics, you are sure to have a visually appealing quilt.

The fabrics on the following pages are friends you need to get to know.

Tone-on-Tones

Tone-on-tone prints are supporters. These neutral-feeling fabrics make your other fabrics look great. I like to use tone-on-tone prints for backgrounds and faces. For ideas, look at the gold tone-on-tone prints in "You Are the Sun, Moon, and Stars to Me" (page 17). Your fabric stash should include lots of tone-on-tone prints.

Plaids

When you work with plaids, you find that they have different roles in design. Tone-on-tone plaids have a tranquil feel, while plaids with bolder lines have graphic, dramatic appeal. You can use the different values in plaids to add drama and personality.

Not every fabric can be a star. Tone-on-tone plaids, like tone-on-tone prints, are often perfect for the supporting cast in folk quilts. (Plaid fabrics are great for backgrounds.) Because plaids are usually made with a lot of light and/or dark-colored threads, their colors are diluted or defused. Plaids are perfect with any fabric: themes, spots, graphics, stripes, and lightgivers. I buy a lot of plaids!

Themes

Theme or conversational prints are everyone's favorite fabrics. These beauties portray fish, food, farms, ferns, frogs, and nearly every other subject. Theme fabrics are fun for borders, in blocks, and cut as appliqué pieces to support your story. Don't make the mistake of using these for backgrounds. Theme fabrics are usually too busy. Also, beware of using too many theme prints. Your eye needs a place to rest. Too many theme prints can ruin a good thing.

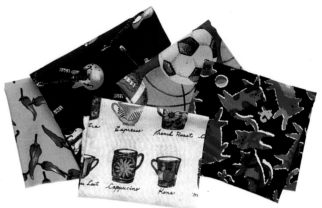

Spots, Dots, or Circles

As you might guess from "Audubon Angel" (page 49), spots, dots, and circles are my favorite shapes. I'm always on the lookout for more when I travel. These prints provide spots of color, great shapes, and zip. Cut in half, they look like little smiles. And they mix wonderfully with plaids and stripes, providing a nice change for your eye. I think spots, dots, and circles are a must for folk quilts.

Graphics

Graphic prints include squares, rectangles, triangles, and other weird shapes that are bold and fun. I used graphic prints to give the first border in "Collectibles" (page 23) texture and dimension. Mixed with plaids, stripes, and dots, graphics add color and interest to scrappy quilts.

Lightgivers

Lightgivers are the best-kept secret in town. These prints include light, medium, and dark values. The light values pull your eye into that portion of the fabric, which is great if you move the fabric around your quilt. Lightgivers take away a lot of the work. Happily, more and more of these fabrics are showing up in quilt shops.

Stripes

Many quilters either avoid or don't understand the value of striped fabric. You can use stripes to direct the eye toward any part of the quilt or cut them off-grain for fun and interest. Striped prints make great tree trunks, legs, house trim, animals, sun rays, and so on. And I'm always on the lookout for striped prints with both light and dark values. These pull the eye into the design. See the creative things stripes can do?

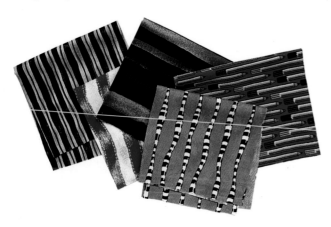

Adding Figures

You can appliqué, fuse, or buttonhole-stitch figures to your quilt top. I hand appliqué my figures. I prefer appliqué to fusing because I want my quilts to be around as long as possible. Fused edges fray over time, and I'm not fond of the stiff feel they give my quilts. But do I have fused quilts in my home? Yes, I do. These are pretty, decorator quilts that probably won't be fashionable ten years down the road, and I won't feel bad about giving them away. I can't say the same of quilts that have bits of my life appliquéd into the fibers.

This is all a matter of taste and opinion, and I would not argue with any quilter who wanted to do all of their creative quilts using fusible web. If you are stretching your creativity, I salute you, whatever method you may choose.

I know some of you are afraid of appliqué, but I encourage you to stick with it. I didn't start with good appliqué skills, but I didn't let that stop me. Luckily, the more appliqué I do, the better I get. If I had listened to some of my well-intentioned guild members, I would have given up appliqué a long time ago. Do what is best for you, and don't let anyone discourage you. You'll find that, with practice, you'll become more proficient too.

Adding Photo Transfers

A picture is worth a thousand words. I've been experimenting with photo transfers for the past few years, and I love how I can use them to include friends and family in my quilts.

I've tried photo-transfer methods such as liquids and iron-on mending tape, but my favorite is iron-on transfer paper (see "Resources" on page 85). This is an inexpensive and easy way to transfer photos.

Read the following instructions carefully. Iron-on transfer paper was originally intended for use with a T-shirt iron, which uses higher heat and pressure than we have at home.

1. Take your original photo and paper to a copy shop. Ask for one copy at a time so the paper doesn't stick together as it goes through the copier. Be sure to copy on the coated (unprinted) side of the paper. Your copy shop may be able to colorize black-and-white photos to match your fabric. Be sure to take a fabric sample.

2. Turn your iron to the highest heat setting (linen) and wait for it to reach maximum heat.

3. Pile a few layers of newspaper on a hard surface. Lay a piece of cloth over the newspaper for a barrier. This is your pressing board.

   Note: Do not use your ironing board; it has too much padding. The padding will prevent you from using enough pressure to make a good imprint.

4. Lay a piece of white or light-colored cotton on the pressing surface. This is the transfer fabric. Position the transfer paper, photo side down, on the fabric.

5. Starting in one corner and using as much pressure as you can, press the iron across the transfer paper. Slowly count to 3, move the iron a few inches, and repeat. When you have pressed the entire paper, gently glide the iron across the entire surface (without applying pressure).

6. Remove the transfer paper while the paper and image are still hot. Starting with one corner, peel the paper off the fabric. If the paper is hard to remove, it was not hot enough. Reheat the image and remove excess paper. If the transferred image is fuzzy, you did not use enough heat or pressure.

Your fabric photo is washable. Iron with medium pressure to restore color after washing.

Adding Words and Letters

Say it loud, say it proud. Words do so much for a quilt! I've always been drawn to old quilts embellished with words and wishes, and I wish there were more. I love to know what the quilters were feeling. There's nothing like words to portray messages of love, sadness, celebration, and the many other emotions that we experience daily.

I often include things my kids say, songs, Bible verses, banter, or poems to support my quilt themes. Simple words such as *buttons, daughter, love,* and *rummage sale* tell us what you think is important and how you felt as you made this quilt.

There are many different methods for adding words to a quilt. I encourage you to try each of these so you'll have a variety of techniques from which to choose.

Appliqué: I think this is the easiest method. I draw my letters on freezer paper, cut them out, then iron the freezer-paper letters to the right side of the fabric. Next, I cut out the letters, leaving a ¼"-wide seam allowance for appliqué. Finally, I clip around curves, remove the freezer paper, and appliqué the letters to the background fabric.

Piecing: There are quite a few patterns and books for pieced letters. I find these attractive and fun, but not as free or as fancy as appliquéd letters. I experimented with piecing my own letters, exaggerating them to make them folksy and whimsical. You may want to try using foundation-pieced letters.

Reverse Appliqué: I like using reverse appliqué with script or curved letters. For examples, look at "In the Beginning" (page 22), "Folk Town" (page 24), and "Let Us Give Thanks" (page 51).

In this method, you stitch fabric for the letters behind your quilt background, cut the letters from your quilt, then appliqué the edges. Cutting up your quilt this way can be scary, but you get nice, sharp-looking letters. You may want to piece the letter fabric to add interest and color.

Begin by tracing your letters on the quilt top. (I prefer using a chalk marking pencil.) Be sure to place your quilt top on a hard surface so you can make neat letters. Carefully cut out the insides of the letters, leaving a ¼"-wide seam allowance. Clip curves and corners. Letters such as *A* and *O* have centers that you will need to sew on later. Turn under the letter edges and appliqué.

Strips: I enjoy using this method for verses or sentences. For an example, look at the outer border of "Folk Ark" (page 28).

Cut fabric strips twice the size of your desired letters, turn the long edges to the back (similar to bias tape), and press. I fold the strips on my quilt, pin them in place, and then appliqué.

Rubber Stamps: These are great for small projects. For an example, look at "Friends from Afar" (page 59).

I get better results using a fabric pen to ink the stamp than using a stamp pad. After the stamped area has dried, use a hot iron to set the ink.

Cyanotype Fabric: These fabrics, which are available in several colors, react to sunlight. I prefer buying the fabric by the yard rather than in precut kits (see "Resources" on page 85). This is an easy and fun method for adding letters and images to your quilts. For an example, look at "Cajun Katy Loves Bayou Bob" (page 55). For best results, follow the directions closely.

Make stick-on letters from Con-Tact® paper or buy these at an office-supply store, place them on the fabric, and expose the fabric to the sun as directed by the manufacturer (usually no longer than 10 minutes).

Broderie Perse: Broderie perse is the name of an old method for cutting printed images from one fabric and appliquéing them on another. Look for fabrics printed with words or images. Simply cut out the letters or images, leaving a ¼"-wide seam allowance to turn under if desired, then hand or machine appliqué.

Stencils: There are many stencil patterns available through quilt shops, craft stores, and catalogs, but I prefer making my own using freezer paper. (I recommend Reynolds® freezer paper. This brand is a nice weight and responds well to heat.) For an example, look at "When Pigs Fly" (page 57).

I like to use fabric paint for stenciling. Most fabric paints don't affect the hand of the fabric as much as craft paints. For best results, use dark paint on lighter background fabrics. Light paint often won't show up on a dark background fabric.

I stencil the letters on the fabric before piecing it into the quilt top. Begin by drawing or tracing letters onto freezer paper. (Make sure the letters are the right size for the quilt top.) Cut out the insides of the letters, making sure the edges are crisp and neat.

Position the stencil on your fabric and press (use a cotton or high-heat setting). Make sure the freezer-paper stencil is firmly attached to the fabric so paint cannot seep under the edges.

Dip a foam brush in fabric paint and dab excess paint on a paper towel. When you're stenciling, less is more. Avoid loading the brush and fabric with paint. Gently dab or swirl paint in the letters. When the paint is dry, remove the stencil. (If you remove the stencil before the paint dries, you may smudge the lettering.) Heat-set the paint as directed by the manufacturer.

Quilting

Many quilters ask me whether I prefer hand or machine quilting. The quilts my grandmothers made were always hand quilted, and I was brought up with the idea that no quilt worth anything was machine quilted. In the 1980s, I realized there was no way I could hand quilt as many quilts as I was making. I needed someone to machine quilt for me (someone who could keep up with me).

I found several machine quilters in my area, but I guess I wore them out. Eventually, I found Pam Clarke. I simply hand my quilt tops over to Pam and she quilts them as her creativity leads her. I've never been disappointed in her work, and she says working this way has helped her grow creatively.

I still hand quilt one quilt per year, and there's no hand sewing I enjoy more.

Embellishing

Embellishments add color, texture, and eye appeal to your quilts. Do you feel like you need embellishment ideas? (When I talk about embellishments, I don't mean just buttons.) My favorites include:

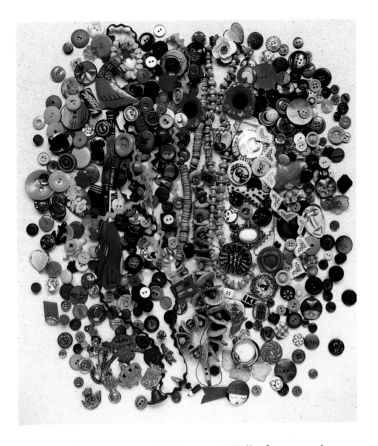

4-H buttons, ribbons, and pins

awards and ribbons of any kind

ballet slippers

beads

Boy Scout memorabilia

buttons

Camp Fire memorabilia

cigarette silks

clothing collars

clothing labels

Cracker Jack charms

craft sticks

fake fingernails

fake fruit

firefighter trivia

fishing lures

flosses

game pieces

garters

Girl Scout memorabilia

hairpins, barrettes, and mini-curlers

hankies

hardware-store finds

kids' plastic jewelry

lace

metal charms

nurses' hats

nutshells

old jewelry

old watch parts

party favors

pins

plastic bugs and spiders

plastic rings

poker chips

police trivia

purse closures

raffia

religious medallions

rickrack

sequins

silk flowers

snaps

T-shirt logos

toy clickers

twigs

uniform patches

union buttons

whistles

wooden cutouts

wooden nickels

How do you use embellishments? Well, if you saved your child's red plastic necklace with dogs and cats, use it to embellish a quilt with your child's name and dog or cat figures. Does your husband love to fish? What fisherman wouldn't love having his BIG catch memorialized? Embellish the quilt with flies and lures. Do make sure he's willing to part with the ones you want to use. And remember to remove the hooks before you sew them on!

The possibilities are infinite. The beauty of embellishment is that the items you include will be treasured for years to come rather than stuck in an attic somewhere.

"No one can arrive from being talented alone. God gives talent, work transforms talent into genius."

ANNA PAVLOVA

Questions and Answers

It's easy to attach beads and buttons, but you may have items that are trickier to use. There's no need to panic. Something in the following question-and-answer section should help you solve the problem.

QUESTION: *Should buttons, beads, and other items be sewn on before quilting or after?*

ANSWER: Sewing embellishments on after quilting works best. The weight of the embellishments may stress the fabric. After quilting, you can sew through all three layers of the quilt. This helps stabilize the whole quilt, especially the heavily embellished areas.

QUESTION: *What if I want to use an item that doesn't have a hole in it?*

ANSWER: Buy yourself a drill. Embellishments made from wood or soft plastic are fairly easy to drill. For metal, you may need a stronger, heavy-duty drill bit. *Warning:* If your embellishment seems too dense, it may be too heavy to hang from a quilt. Some things put too much stress on a small area of the quilt. In this case, find something else.

QUESTION: *Can I add more than one type of embellishment to an area without making it look overdone?*

ANSWER: Yes! For an example, look at "Tea for Two" on page 36. I drilled holes through walnut shells and sewed on red buttons to look like small cherries on cookies. To complete the illusion, I used red jewels for jelly and old celluloid buttons for candies. If I'd used fabric to make the goodies, the quilt would not be as interesting.

QUESTION: *What problems have you had with embellishments?*

ANSWER: The main trouble spots are listed below.

- **Washing:** This can be a problem. Hand washing usually works well, but some embellishments may bleed or stain your quilt if you wash them. If you use metal buttons, red buttons, painted wooden items, or dark embroidery floss, you risk rust and dye stains when you wash the quilt. Instead, hang these quilts and lightly go over them with a dry terry cloth towel—avoiding the embellishments—to remove dust.

Some of my quilts include family treasures that I know can't be laundered. I keep these out of direct sun and light. Because I want these quilts and embellishments to be seen and enjoyed by family, friends, and especially myself, I live with the fact that they're not washable.

- **Weight:** If your embellishment is too heavy, you risk tearing or stretching your quilt fabric. To test this, cut a square of cotton, batting, and backing. Baste the layers together. Sew your embellishment to your test quilt and hang it somewhere for a week. If the embellishment stretches the fabric or distorts the test quilt, don't use it.

- **Overdoing it:** Some themes cry out for more embellishment; for others, more is simply too much. Think about which approach is best before you start sewing on your treasures. As a general rule, don't make the embellishments the story. Instead, use your embellishments to highlight your theme.

- **Strength:** I've seen embellishments literally hanging from quilts by a thread. For sewing embellishments, use a heavy thread such as quilting or button thread. Use short lengths of thread; this keeps it from fraying and breaking. Sew through embellishments at least twice so they're secure.

I avoid using glue on my quilts. It's difficult to tell how long glue will hold or whether it may rot the fabric. On the other hand, it's your quilt. If you want to use glue, then use it.

When I include family jewelry or other embellishments that I don't want to risk losing, I attach these to the unquilted top, then glue the pin back closed or the earring shank to the backing. (I use Super Glue™.) I make sure the glue only comes in contact with the jewelry. So far, I have not lost any of these treasured pieces. I can't say that of some of the things I did not glue.

PART FIVE

IN CONCLUSION,
MY CREATIVE FRIENDS

My Creative Friends Challenge Quilt #1, blocks by (left to right) Patricia Donahue-O'Boyle, Linda Hunt, Jackie Anderson, Katherine Parry, Tracy McHugh, Kathy Skomer, Judy Goodrich, Chris Bristow, Candy Huddleston, RaeLynn Roadhouse, Terry Waldron, Carol Scott, Manya Powell, Linda Sullivan, Tiffany Burrows, and Lisa Valentine, 1996, Spokane, Washington, 77" x 101". Assembled by Manya Powell. Machine quilted by Pam Clarke.

> "*A true friend is someone who is there for you when he would rather be somewhere else.*"
> LEN WEIN

My Creative Friends Challenge Quilt #2, blocks by (left to right) Shauna Stewart, Manya Powell, Michelene Svanda, Candy Huddleston, Julie Lynch, JoAnn Kliewer, Manya Powell, Pam Clarke, Jean Vinson, Joan Hodgebloom, Melody Coffey-Love, Beth Warren, Debbie Hodin, Mollie Ressa, Becky Lyden, and Barbara Lambrecht, 1995, Spokane, Washington, 70½" x 98½". Assembled by Mary Lou Weidman. Machine quilted by Pam Clarke.

The more I teach creativity, the more I hear the same lament. Students want to make creative quilts, but because they don't feel they are creative, they are afraid to try. We are all creative, we just need to learn, or relearn, how to use our creativity. The best way to accomplish this is to push yourself out of your comfort zone.

To prove this, I sent a creative block challenge to fifty quilting friends. I made sure to include a variety of different skill levels and experience—from talented shop owners to beginners who had only made the simplest blocks. I knew that if these quilters took up my challenge, I would see a variety of finished blocks. The results were wonderful, and delighted not only me but my quilting friends and family.

This is the letter I sent:

My Creative Friend,

I am sending you this letter because you are a creative and inspirational friend. Here is a simple idea for a Creative Friend block challenge.

The challenge is to take the dimensions needed for the Creative Friend block and to do with it whatever you wish. By changing the dimensions of the hat, head, and shoulders, you can get different looks. By making a small hat, for example, you could have a large beard. By changing the height and width of a hat, you could get many varied looks and personalities.

All blocks need to be 10½" x 18½" finished.

You may want to think about characters such as a keystone cop, a princess, a cowboy, a Victorian lady, a nurse, a scarecrow, a farmer, etc. Please add faces, hair, and details to hats and body.

Embellishments are a welcome addition. Piecing any features could be even more interesting and fun. Don't forget, friends come in all colors.

Good luck and thank you for taking the challenge!

Mary Lou Weidman

Some blocks came back immediately, while others took more time. Some quilters had to be coaxed and encouraged. A couple of friends were begged. Did they have fun? Most everyone said it was a lot of fun, and easier once they got started. So often, we talk ourselves out of challenges, not realizing what this can do for our creativity muscles. (Kind of like putting off exercise.) To show you how others work, I've included comments from some of the quilters and their blocks on the following pages.

SELF-PORTRAIT

by Melody Coffey-Love

WITCH

by Judy Goodrich

What does she do? What is she like? How can I say everything with cloth? Where do I start? I had many questions, and all the answers kept coming back to me. My creative friend should be a caricature of me.

Oh, those great earrings I bought in Hawaii … they are too gaudy for the "real" me to wear, but perfect for this! She'll have to have wild hair (like mine) in shades of brown, gray, and blonde.

She must wear those great '50s-style glasses I got at a garage sale; they'll be perfect! They remind me of the glasses I used to wear in grade school.

Once I started, I really got carried away. My self-portrait ended up to be the woman my children fear I'll become if I lose complete control. She's not the real me, but the parts of me that are eccentric, funny, and care-free—the parts of my personality that encourage creativity and inventiveness. This was really fun! It's good to laugh at yourself sometimes. It puts life in perspective.

When I received Mary Lou's challenge, I was flattered that she thought of me as a creative friend. I'd never hand appliquéd (I'd always avoided attempting it), but I didn't want to be left out!

I decided to make a witch. I looked through lots of magazines and books to find a look I could turn into a block. When I doodle, I often draw profiles of goofy-looking people. This could work for my block. The hand appliqué went slowly, but I'm pleased with the results. Since making this block, I've started an appliqué quilt for a friend.

TRADITIONAL JAPANESE WOMAN

by JoAnn Funakoshi Kliewer

SELF-PORTRAIT

by Candy Huddleston

My first thought, as I considered creating a person with a hat, was to do something with a Japanese look. This block is based on a traditional image of a Japanese woman. The hair ornaments served as a hat. Creating something without a pattern seemed at first intimidating, but was fun and rewarding. It gave me the confidence and the desire to create more "original" work.

My creativity can be triggered by many things. For instance, the idea for my coat came from a bag of purple corduroy scraps I bought at a garage sale. And since I am known for liking purple and other bright colors, the stocking-hat brim had to be yellow. Doll hair made perfect braids. I couched metallic gold cording on my glasses, then glued on small pearls for a faux zipper. I always look for odds and ends at garage sales because I never know what will trigger my next creativity attack.

SELF-PORTRAIT (BIRD BRAIN)

by Barbara Lambrecht

I'm someone who can rise to a challenge, and Mary Lou's project sparked my enthusiasm. I wanted to create a face that was different from all the others, one that said something. I also wanted to add humor, something I learned from Mary Lou's workshop. At home, we joke about which hat we're wearing today: farmers, ranchers, or construction workers. My self-portrait evolved from this idea. I combined my love of bluebirds with my favorite cowboy hat. My husband entitled it "Bird Brain."

THE GEOLOGIST

by Manya Powell

I love a challenge. When Mary Lou asked me to do a Creative Friend block, I was thrilled.

When I am working on an idea for a project, I like to let it simmer in my mind for awhile. Usually, a great solution will present itself. I originally wanted to make a self-portrait, but I decided I looked too boring. Next, I thought Mary Lou probably needed some men in her blocks, so I decided to do an outdoor type. I thought he would probably be in the forest near us, so I wanted a leafy background. He should be wearing a flannel shirt, of course, and would have a beard. The best hair/beard fabric in my stash was a mix of browns and reds. By the time I finished, this gentleman looked just like my husband, the geologist. Especially his nose!

MATRUSHKA DOLL

by Manya Powell

FISH-FACE

by Manya Powell

With "The Geologist," I was just getting warmed up. My daughter suggested a Matrushka doll because we collect them. I got out one of our dolls and did my best to translate it into a design for a quilt block. Once I'd chosen some ethnic-type fabrics from my stash, I started sewing.

My next block idea came about because we play "fish-face" with our kids. Our doormat is decorated with a salmon, and one day, I looked at it and just knew Mary Lou needed a Fish-Face block. I tried to draw only the face of the fish, so it would go with the other faces. I used wild fabrics on this one, and it came together pretty fast.

OK, enough is enough. I had a great time with these blocks. They are totally different from any quilt block I've experimented with before. There are a lot more ideas in my head, just waiting to pop out.

SCUBA DIVER

by Terry Waldron

Sometimes creativity comes when you least expect it, but need it most. After I started my original block (and bragged about it to my friends), I realized I was doing it wrong. I started a whole body instead of a head. I sat down in the middle of the floor and started grabbing fabric (that's where I start). Because I panicked, I picked vivid oranges and laid them on a stand-and-deliver turquoise. Then I grabbed peach fabric and started cutting.

Soon there was a diver staring back at me, and I don't know how or why! The bubbles just had to go up in a curve toward the surface because everything else was circles and arcs. The look on his face? That's my self-portrait. It is exactly the way I felt the whole time I was sewing. The adrenaline rush was fun!

Creative Friends Exercise

You can see how differently everyone approached this challenge. I've included two face patterns (pages 90–95) so you can try it yourself. Quilters often shy away from making people, but this is a no-threat approach. (This is an exercise I plan to work on for my creative family quilt.) I know you are creative and can do something really fun and wonderful with this idea. To help you a little more, I've also included creative ideas for eyes, noses, and mouths (pages 83–84).

Before you begin your block, look through your fabrics. Think about how you can adapt patterns and shaded areas like I've done at right. A rose-print fabric provides perfectly wild eyes, and a desert scene becomes a sensuous, pouty mouth. By focusing on this idea and using your imagination, you can create wonderful and unique faces.

Look for patterns and shaded areas you can adapt for your block.

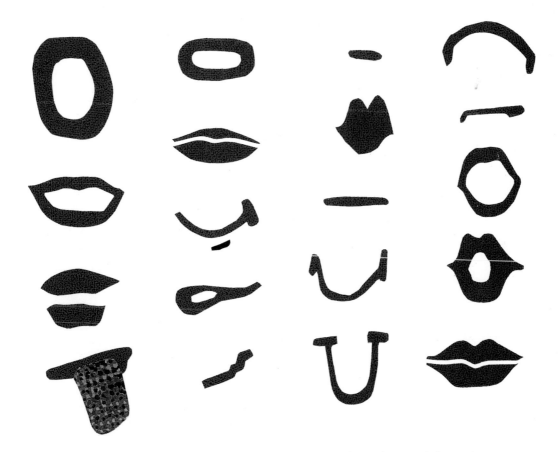

A smile, a smirk, a grin, a look of surprise: mouth shapes are another way to communicate your story.

The eyes say it all. Try varying eye shape and color, and adding eyebrows.

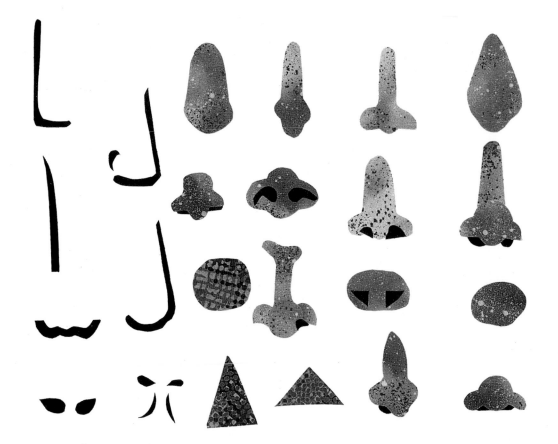

Have you ever taken a really good look at noses? The variety of shapes and forms seems infinite.

Conclusion

I hope this book has given you new insights into and creative ideas for your work. Remember, you have everything you need to make original and unique quilts. It's up to you to move forward on the path to creativity.

Below is a little analogy to all that is creative in itself. My grandfather wrote this poem many years ago, and it expresses what I want to say to you in closing.

> Welcome, stranger, to my cabin if this way
>   you chance to pass.
> On the door there is no padlock, there's no need
>   to break the glass.
> Are you cold? You will find kindling
>   whittled neatly in the box.
> If your feet are wet and tired, help yourself
>   to woolen socks.
> Chances are that you are hungry,
>   in the larder have a look.
> Mine are simple tastes but plenty,
>   all you have to do is cook.
> Use the bed if you are sleepy,
>   may your dreams all happy end.
> Here's to better luck tomorrow,
> Cheerio, my unknown friend.

LEN FLESBERG, WARDNER,
BRITISH COLUMBIA, CANADA

I wish you all of life's best, creatively.

Meet the Artist

Mary Lou Donahue Weidman has a background in Fine Arts and likes to dabble in every art medium. Mary Lou learned to quilt in 1974 and began quilting in earnest during her son's cancer treatments two years later. Mary Lou made her first folk-style story quilt in 1987, combining her art background and creativity to come up with her popular style.

Mary Lou's goal is to teach others how to recapture their creativity and create their own best efforts. "Every event in life is a quilt waiting to happen."

Mary Lou lives in Spokane, Washington, with her husband, Mark; daughter Shelbi; and the family dog, Louie.

Bibliography

Amabaile, Teresa M., Ph.D. *Growing Up Creative, Nurturing a Lifetime of Creativity.* New York: Crown Publishers, Inc., 1989.

Bono, Edward. *Serious Creativity: Using the Power of Lateral Thinking to Create New Ideas.* New York: Harper Business, 1992.

Von Oech, Roger. *A Whack on the Side of the Head.* New York: Warner, 1983.

Resources

Blueprints Printables
1504 #7 Industrial Way
Belmont, CA 94002
1-800-356-0445
Cyanotype fabric

Dharma Trading Company
Box 150916
San Rafael, CA 94915
1-800-542-5227 or (415)
456-7657
Iron-on transfer paper

In The Beginning Fabrics
8201 Lake City Way NE
Seattle, WA 98115
1-206-523-1121
Fabric by Mary Lou Weidman

ala mode OUT-TAKES
Mary Lou

When I started teaching on a regular basis, I decided to attach a recipe to my class handouts just for fun. I didn't realize how important those recipes would become. Some of my students said they took my class again for the recipe! I've had quite a few former students call and ask me for recipes they lost and needed for special occasions. I'm including a few of the recipes I've given to my classes (again, just for fun). These recipes are not for the diet-conscious, but they're a good reason to cheat. Enjoy!

PATCHWORK PIZZA

Family and friends love this recipe. A number of students called for it at the request of their families.

1 pound boneless chicken breasts

3 cloves garlic, minced

2 tablespoons rice vinegar

2 tablespoons fresh lemon juice

2 tablespoons soy sauce

½ teaspoon ground black pepper

½ cup green onion, sliced

2 tablespoons olive oil

1 heaping tablespoon cornstarch

1 large pizza crust (I use Boboli®.)

½ yellow onion, sliced and sautéed

½ to 1 whole red, green, or yellow bell pepper, chopped

¾ cup Monterey Jack cheese, shredded

½ cup mozzarella cheese, shredded

1 zucchini, sliced

¼ cup pine nuts or chopped almonds

Cut chicken into ½" pieces. In a large glass or plastic bowl, combine garlic, vinegar, lemon juice, soy sauce, black pepper, and half of the green onion with 1 tablespoon of the olive oil. Add chicken and stir to coat. Let stand 30 minutes at room temperature. Drain, reserving the marinade.

Preheat oven to 400°F. Heat remaining oil in large skillet over medium heat; add chicken. Cook 3 to 4 minutes over medium heat or until no longer pink. Stir cornstarch into marinade. Add to skillet. Cook and stir until thick and bubbly. Spoon onto pizza crust. Top with yellow onion and bell pepper, then cheeses.

Bake at 400°F for 12 minutes. Remove from the oven and add zucchini, nuts, and remaining green onion. Return to oven and bake for 2 minutes. This is very filling pizza. Serves 6 as a main dish.

"It isn't so much what's on the table that matters, as what's on the chairs."

W. S. GILBERT

MARION MORRISON'S CURRIED FRUIT BAKE

Marion is our adopted family member and my mother's best friend. This recipe, which is wonderful served with brunch, lunch, or dinner, is a part of every family gathering.

1½ cups brown sugar

2 tablespoons butter, melted

1 tablespoon curry powder

2 tablespoons cornstarch

1 tablespoon lemon juice

16-oz. can each of pear, apricot, pineapple, and peach halves or slices in syrup, drained (reserve juice)

¾ cup apricot juice (from canned fruit)

¾ cup pineapple juice (from canned fruit)

Small jar of maraschino cherries, drained

Preheat oven to 325°F. Combine brown sugar, butter, curry powder, cornstarch, lemon juice, fruits, and fruit juice. Spread in 2-quart baking dish. Bake uncovered for 1 hour. Add cherries before serving. Use a slotted spoon to serve or place in individual bowls. Serves 8.

MARY LOU'S CHOCOLATE PATCHWORK CHEESECAKE

1 package (1¼ lbs.) chocolate sandwich cookies (such as Oreo® or Hydrox®)

⅓ cup butter or margarine, melted

4 packages (8 oz. each) cream cheese, softened and cut into chunks

1 cup sugar

⅓ cup whipping cream

6 large eggs

2 tablespoons all-purpose flour

1 tablespoon vanilla extract

Preheat oven to 300°F. In a food processor or blender, whirl half the package of cookies, including filling, until you have fine crumbs. (If using a blender, grind only about 5 cookies at a time and empty into bowl.) Add melted butter and blend. Scoop crumbs into a 9"-diameter springform pan. Press crumbs evenly over bottom of pan and halfway up the sides. Chill until firm (about 20 minutes).

In food processor or using an electric mixer, beat cream cheese, sugar, and cream until smooth. Add eggs, flour, and vanilla. Blend well.

Pour half of cheesecake mixture into chilled crust. Break remaining cookies in half and scatter over the mixture, overlapping cookies if necessary to use them all. Pour remaining mixture over cookies.

Bake about 1 hour and 20 minutes, until cheesecake is golden and jiggles only slightly in the center when shaken. Cool. Chill the cheesecake at least 4 hours before serving. Serves 12 to 16.

In the summer, I garnish the cheesecake with fresh strawberries. In the winter, I serve it with a dollop or two of cherry-pie filling.

CANADIAN PHOENIX BARS

Several years ago, I met Canadian sisters Kay Parker and Doreen Angus in Phoenix, Arizona. These amazing ladies quilt, entertain like Martha Stewart, and bake like pros. I'm sure they are some of Canada's national treasures, as is this recipe which they graciously shared.

¼ pound plus 6 tablespoons (1¾ sticks) butter

¼ cup light Karo syrup

½ cup raisins

1¼ cups flour

1 teaspoon baking powder

1 cup coconut

½ cup sugar

1¼ cups cornflake cereal, crushed

Preheat the oven to 350°F. Place butter and Karo syrup in a heavy saucepan over medium heat until butter is melted. Remove from heat. Add raisins. Sift flour and baking powder into saucepan. Add coconut, sugar, and crushed cornflakes. Mix thoroughly, then press into a greased 9" x 13" pan. Bake for 15 minutes. While the bars cool, prepare lemon icing:

2 cups powdered sugar

2 teaspoons grated fresh lemon rind

1 tablespoon butter

2 tablespoons fresh lemon juice (or more as needed)

Mix all ingredients until smooth. Spread icing on cool bars.

AUNT LU'S "DON'T GIVE THIS RECIPE TO ANYONE" FUDGE

This recipe is from my great aunt, also a great cook. A special holiday fudge, it's well worth the effort.

4 cups sugar

1 cup light Karo syrup

1 cup butter

4 ounces unsweetened chocolate

4 cups whipping cream, divided

1 teaspoon real vanilla extract

2 cups walnuts

Combine sugar, Karo syrup, butter, chocolate, and 2 cups cream in a heavy saucepan. Bring to a boil, stirring constantly. Boil 15 minutes. Reduce heat. Gradually add remaining cream, stirring constantly. Cook for about 1 hour, until the candy reaches 234°F (soft-ball stage). Add vanilla and beat until thick. Stir in nuts. Spread in 9" x 13" pan. Let cool; cut into squares.

TEMPLATES

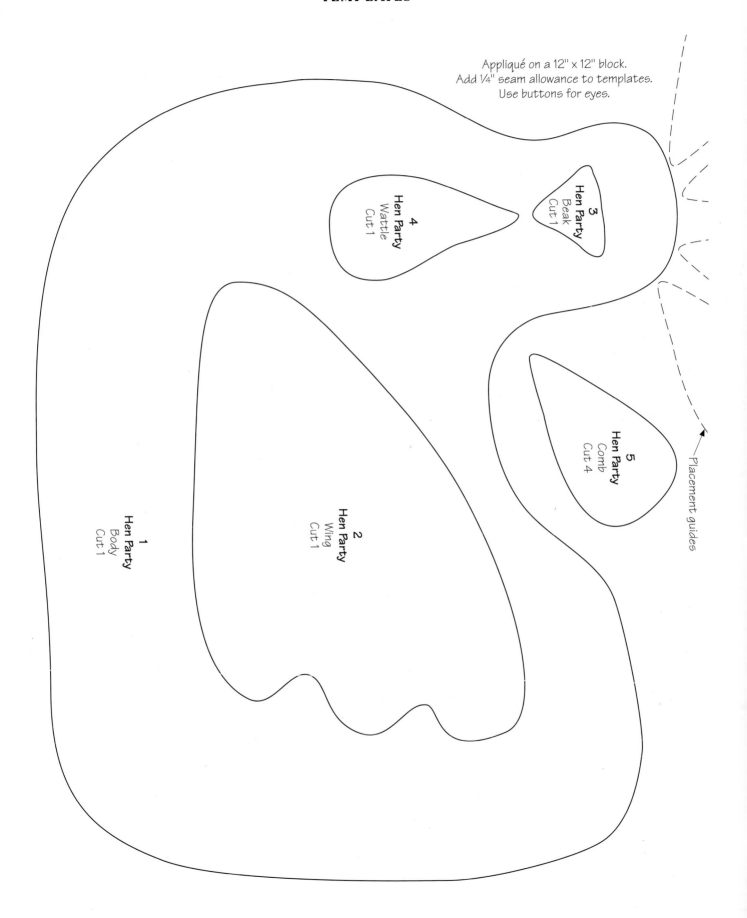

Appliqué on a 12" x 12" block.
Add ¼" seam allowance to templates.
Use buttons for eyes.

3
Hen Party
Beak
Cut 1

4
Hen Party
Wattle
Cut 1

5
Hen Party
Comb
Cut 4

Placement guides

2
Hen Party
Wing
Cut 1

1
Hen Party
Body
Cut 1

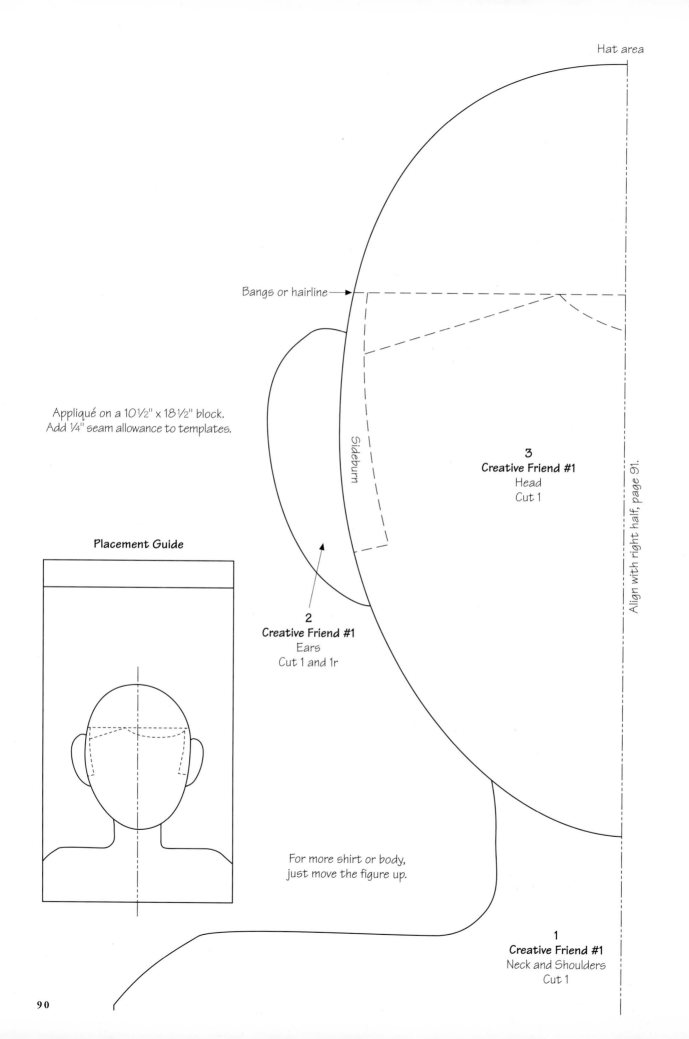

Hat area

Bangs or hairline →

Sideburn

Appliqué on a 10½" x 18½" block.
Add ¼" seam allowance to templates.

3
Creative Friend #1
Head
Cut 1

Align with right half, page 91.

Placement Guide

2
Creative Friend #1
Ears
Cut 1 and 1r

For more shirt or body,
just move the figure up.

1
Creative Friend #1
Neck and Shoulders
Cut 1

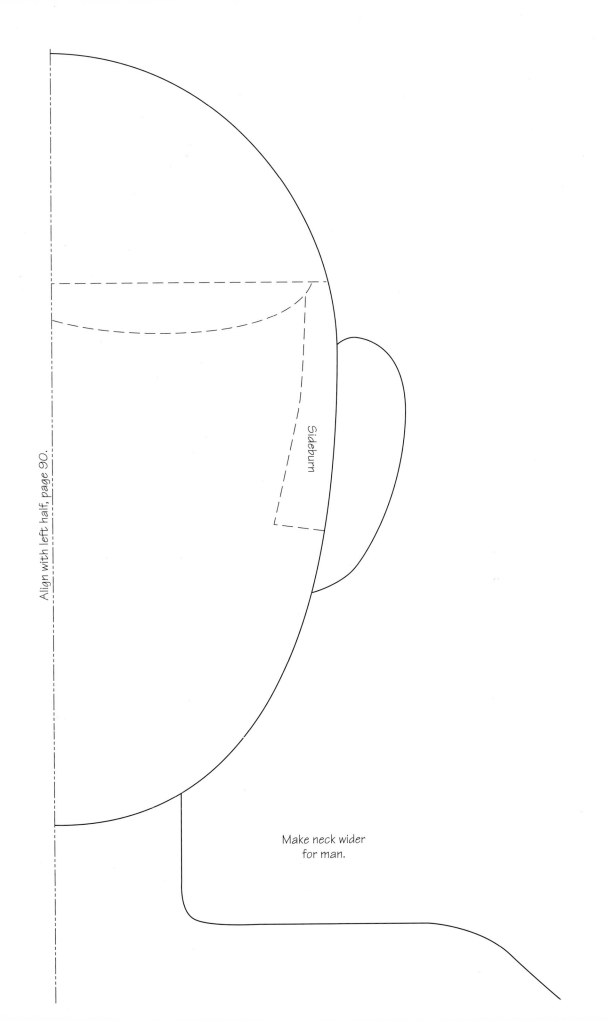

Align with left half, page 90.

Sideburn

Make neck wider
for man.

Instructions for piecing Creative Friend block:

1. Sew pieces 1, 2, and 3.
2. Sew piece 4 to the unit made in step 1.
3. Sew pieces 5 and 6, then pieces 7 and 8.
4. Sew pieces 9, 10, and 11.
5. Sew the units made in step 3 to the unit made in step 4.
6. Sew the unit made in step 5 to the unit made in step 2.
7. Sew pieces 12, 13, and 14.
8. Sew pieces 15, 16, and 17.
9. Sew the units made in steps 7 and 8 to the unit made in step 6.
10. Sew piece 18 to the unit made in step 9.

Placement Guide

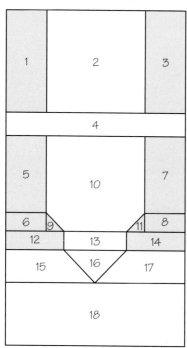

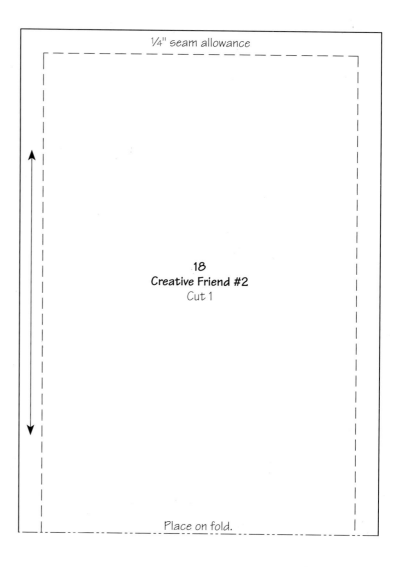

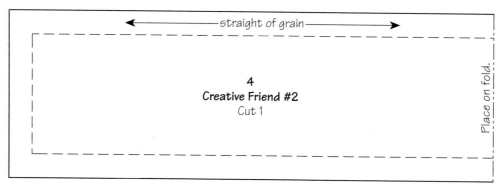

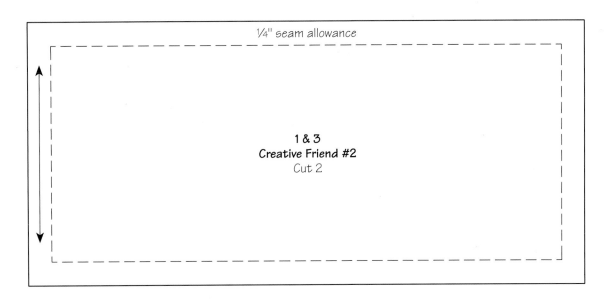

¼" seam allowance

1 & 3
Creative Friend #2
Cut 2

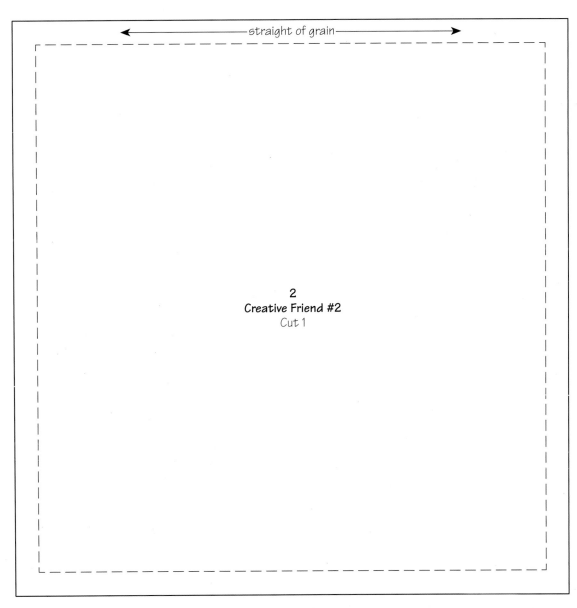

straight of grain

2
Creative Friend #2
Cut 1

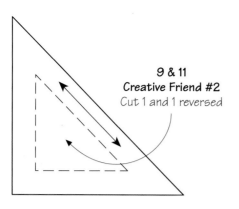

9 & 11
Creative Friend #2
Cut 1 and 1 reversed

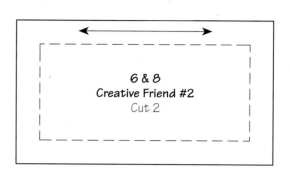

6 & 8
Creative Friend #2
Cut 2

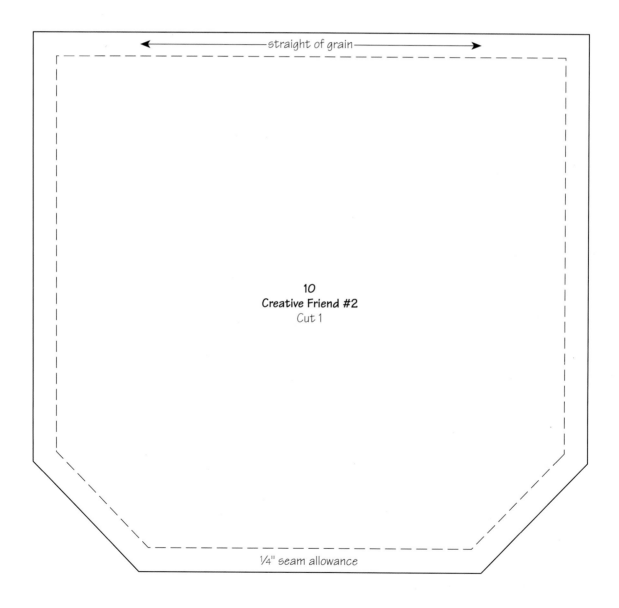

straight of grain

10
Creative Friend #2
Cut 1

¼" seam allowance

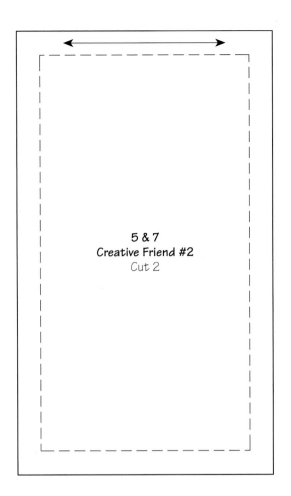

5 & 7
Creative Friend #2
Cut 2

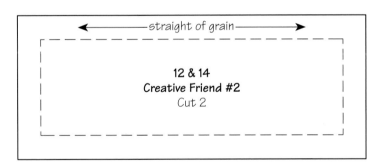

straight of grain

12 & 14
Creative Friend #2
Cut 2

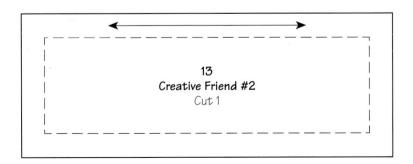

13
Creative Friend #2
Cut 1

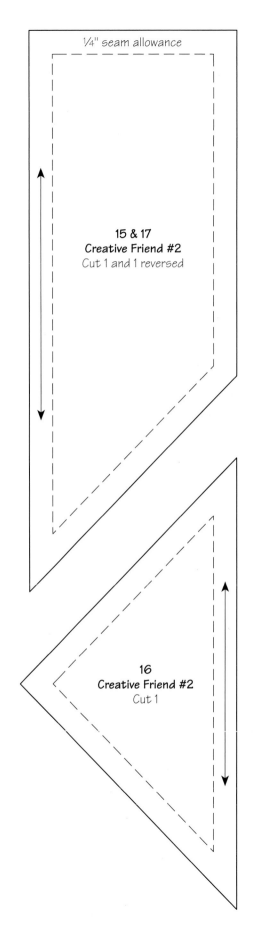

¼" seam allowance

15 & 17
Creative Friend #2
Cut 1 and 1 reversed

16
Creative Friend #2
Cut 1

Publications and Products

THAT PATCHWORK PLACE TITLES:

America's Best-Loved Quilt Books®

All the Blocks Are Geese • Mary Sue Suit
All New Copy Art for Quilters
All-Star Sampler • Roxanne Carter
Angle Antics • Mary Hickey
Appliqué in Bloom • Gabrielle Swain
Appliquilt® • Tonee White
Appliquilt® for Christmas • Tonee White
Appliquilt® to Go • Tonee White
Appliquilt® Your ABCs • Tonee White
Around the Block with Judy Hopkins
At Home with Quilts • Nancy J. Martin
Baltimore Bouquets • Mimi Dietrich
Bargello Quilts • Marge Edie
Beyond Charm Quilts
    • Catherine L. McIntee & Tammy L. Porath
Bias Square® Miniatures • Christine Carlson
Biblical Blocks • Rosemary Makhan
Blockbender Quilts • Margaret J. Miller
Block by Block • Beth Donaldson
Borders by Design • Paulette Peters
Calicoes & Quilts Unlimited
    • Judy Betts Morrison
The Cat's Meow • Janet Kime
Celebrate! with Little Quilts • Alice Berg,
    Sylvia Johnson & Mary Ellen Von Holt
Celebrating the Quilt
Class-Act Quilts
*Classic Quilts with Precise Foundation
    Piecing* • Tricia Lund & Judy Pollard
Colourwash Quilts • Deirdre Amsden
Country Medallion Sampler • Carol Doak
Crazy Rags • Deborah Brunner
Decorate with Quilts & Collections
    • Nancy J. Martin
Down the Rotary Road with Judy Hopkins
Dress Daze • Judy Murrah
The Easy Art of Appliqué
    • Mimi Dietrich & Roxi Eppler
Easy Machine Paper Piecing • Carol Doak
*Easy Mix & Match Machine Paper
    Piecing* • Carol Doak
Easy Paper-Pieced Keepsake Quilts
    • Carol Doak
Easy Reversible Vests • Carol Doak
A Fine Finish • Cody Mazuran
*Five- and Seven-Patch Blocks & Quilts for
    the ScrapSaver* • Judy Hopkins
*Four-Patch Blocks & Quilts for the
    ScrapSaver* • Judy Hopkins
Freedom in Design • Mia Rozmyn
From a Quilter's Garden • Gabrielle Swain
Go Wild with Quilts • Margaret Rolfe
Go Wild with Quilts—Again! • Margaret Rolfe

Great Expectations • Karey Bresenhan
    with Alice Kish & Gay E. McFarland
Hand-Dyed Fabric Made Easy
    • Adriene Buffington
Happy Endings • Mimi Dietrich
Honoring the Seasons • Takako Onoyama
Jacket Jazz • Judy Murrah
Jacket Jazz Encore • Judy Murrah
The Joy of Quilting
    • Joan Hanson & Mary Hickey
Kids Can Quilt • Barbara J. Eikmeier
Little Quilts • Alice Berg, Sylvia Johnson &
    Mary Ellen Von Holt
Lively Little Logs • Donna McConnell
The Log Cabin Design Workbook
    • Christal Carter
Loving Stitches • Jeana Kimball
Machine Quilting Made Easy • Maurine Noble
*Magic Base Blocks for Unlimited Quilt
    Designs* • Patty Barney & Cooky Schock
Miniature Baltimore Album Quilts
    • Jenifer Buechel
Mirror Manipulations • Gail Valentine
More Jazz from Judy Murrah
More Strip-Pieced Watercolor Magic
    • Deanna Spingola
*Nine-Patch Blocks & Quilts for the
    ScrapSaver* • Judy Hopkins
No Big Deal • Deborah L. White
Once upon a Quilt
    • Bonnie Kaster & Virginia Athey
Patchwork Pantry
    • Suzette Halferty & Carol C. Porter
A Perfect Match • Donna Lynn Thomas
A Pioneer Doll and Her Quilts • Mary Hickey
Press for Success • Myrna Giesbrecht
Quilted for Christmas, Book II
Quilted for Christmas, Book III
Quilted Landscapes • Joan Blalock
Quilted Legends of the West
    • Judy Zehner & Kim Mosher
Quilted Sea Tapestries • Ginny Eckley
Quilting Design Sourcebook • Dorothy Osler
Quilting Makes the Quilt • Lee Cleland
Quilting Up a Storm • Lydia Quigley
Quilts: An American Legacy • Mimi Dietrich
Quilts for Baby • Ursula Reikes
Quilts for Red-Letter Days • Janet Kime
Quilts Say It Best • Eileen Westfall
Refrigerator Art Quilts • Jennifer Paulson
Repiecing the Past • Sara Rhodes Dillow
Rotary Riot • Judy Hopkins & Nancy J. Martin
Rotary Roundup
    • Judy Hopkins & Nancy J. Martin
Round Robin Quilts
    • Pat Magaret & Donna Slusser
Sensational Settings • Joan Hanson
Sew a Work of Art Inside and Out
    • Charlotte Bird

*Shortcuts: A Concise Guide to Rotary
    Cutting* • Donna Lynn Thomas
Simply Scrappy Quilts • Nancy J. Martin
Small Talk • Donna Lynn Thomas
Square Dance • Martha Thompson
Start with Squares • Martha Thompson
Strip-Pieced Watercolor Magic
    • Deanna Spingola
Stripples • Donna Lynn Thomas
Sunbonnet Sue All Through the Year
    • Sue Linker
Template-Free® Quilts and Borders
    • Trudie Hughes
Through the Window & Beyond
    • Lynne Edwards
The Total Bedroom • Donna Babylon
Traditional Blocks Meet Appliqué
    • Deborah J. Moffett-Hall
Transitions • Andrea Balosky
True Style • Peggy True
Victorian Elegance • Lezette Thomason
Watercolor Impressions
    • Pat Magaret & Donna Slusser
Watercolor Quilts
    • Pat Magaret & Donna Slusser
Weave It! Quilt It! Wear It!
    • Mary Anne Caplinger
Whimsies & Whynots • Mary Lou Weidman
WOW! Wool-on-Wool Folk Art Quilts
    • Janet Carija Brandt

4", 6", 8" & metric Bias Square® • BiRangle™
Ruby Beholder® • ScrapMaster • Rotary Rule™
Rotary Mate™ • Bias Stripper®
Shortcuts to America's Best-Loved Quilts (video)

FIBER STUDIO PRESS TITLES:

FIBER STUDIO PRESS

Complex Cloth • Jane Dunnewold
*Erika Carter: Personal
    Imagery in Art Quilts* • Erika Carter
Inspiration Odyssey • Diana Swim Wessel
The Nature of Design • Joan Colvin
*Velda Newman: A Painter's Approach
    to Quilt Design* • Velda Newman with
    Christine Barnes

Many titles are available at your local quilt shop.
For more information, write for a free color catalog
to That Patchwork Place, Inc., PO Box 118, Bothell,
WA 98041-0118 USA.

☎ U.S. and Canada, call **1-800-426-3126** for the
name and location of the quilt shop nearest you.
Int'l: 1-206-483-3313   **Fax:** 1-206-486-7596
E-mail: info@patchwork.com
Web: www.patchwork.com   4.97